$54⁵⁰

ASHE Higher Education Report: Volume 41, Number 5
Kelly Ward, Lisa E. Wolf-Wendel, Series Editors

The "Front Porch": Examining the Increasing Interconnection of University and Athletic Department Funding

Jordan R. Bass, Claire C. Schaeperkoetter,

Kyle S. Bunds

D1089502

The "Front Porch": Examining the Increasing Interconnection of
University and Athletic Department Funding
Jordan R. Bass, Claire C. Schaeperkoetter, Kyle S. Bunds
ASHE Higher Education Report: Volume 41, Number 5
Kelly Ward, Lisa E. Wolf-Wendel, Series Editors

Cover image by © iStock.com/stevenfoley

ISSN 1551-6970   electronic ISSN 1554-6306   ISBN 978-1-119-17449-3

The ASHE Higher Education Report is part of the Jossey-Bass Higher and Adult
Education Series and is published six times a year by Wiley Subscription Services,
Inc., A Wiley Company, at Jossey-Bass, One Montgomery Street, Suite 1200, San
Francisco, California 94104-4594.

Individual subscription rate (in USD): $174 per year US/Can/Mex, $210 rest of
world; institutional subscription rate: $352 US, $412 Can/Mex, $463 rest of world.
Single copy rate: $29. Electronic only–all regions: $174 individual, $352
institutional; Print & Electronic–US: $192 individual, $423 institutional; Print &
Electronic–Canada/Mexico: $192 individual, $483 institutional; Print &
Electronic–Rest of World: $228 individual, $534 institutional.

CALL FOR PROPOSALS: Prospective authors are strongly encouraged to contact
Kelly Ward (kaward@wsu.edu) or Lisa E. Wolf-Wendel (lwolf@ku.edu).

Visit the Jossey-Bass Web site at **www.josseybass.com.**

Printed in the United States of America on acid-free recycled paper.

The ASHE Higher Education Report is indexed in CIJE: Current Index to
Journals in Education (ERIC), Education Index/Abstracts (H.W. Wilson), ERIC
Database (Education Resources Information Center), Higher Education Abstracts
(Claremont Graduate University), IBR & IBZ: International Bibliographies of
Periodical Literature (K.G. Saur), and Resources in Education (ERIC).

Advisory Board

Contents

Executive Summary

In this monograph, we broadly examine the cultural and financial relationship between higher education and intercollegiate athletics. A breadth of research on this topic has been conducted over the past half century and will only continue as the expenses of intercollegiate athletics grow at the same time as state support for higher education is waning. In short, we argue the current funding model for intercollegiate athletics is largely unsustainable and may ultimately cause an unhealthy reliance on corporate dollars to fund the big-time athletics machine. Additionally, developments over the last 24 months have only quickened the pace at which changes to the athletics funding structure may need to occur. With each chapter we aim both to aggregate the current literature and critically analyze what practical implications can be garnered from these examinations.

Why Care Now?

We are far from the first set of researchers to attempt this line of inquiry. Murray Sperber (1990, 2000) perhaps most famously put universities under a microscope in *College Sports Inc.: The Athletic Department vs. The University* and *Beer and Circus: How Big-Time College Sports is Crippling Undergraduate Education*. Others like Henry Giroux, Charles Clotfelter, and Taylor Branch have highlighted many of the debates discussed in this text, from the corporatization of intercollegiate athletics and higher education, to the amateur status of college athletes, to name a few. However, over roughly the past half-decade, both academics and popular press journalists have increased the public discourse surrounding the finances of higher education and intercollegiate athletics to unprecedented levels. For example, Colorado State University (CSU) President Tony Frank (2011) stated, "As a university president, I receive input on a wide array of topics, and recently it seems college athletics is on the front burner" (para. 1).

Thus, we argue the plethora of new information and analysis warrants an updated evaluation of the numerous debates surrounding the relationship between higher education and athletics. For example, one popular critique examined in the coming pages is that as financial support for higher education is decreasing in many states, spending on athletics is increasing exponentially. As detailed in the second chapter, the amount of money Rutgers University gave the athletic department during the 2011–2012 school year was enough to hire more than 200 new assistant professors (Eichelberger & Young, 2012). Yet, at the same time many universities are doubling down on their commitment (financial and otherwise) to college athletics and publicly defending the value of sports to their institution. In the same address referenced earlier, CSU's President Frank (2011) goes on to conclude: "CSU—including its reputation—*needs* successful athletic programs" (para. 19, emphasis added). Thus, a great divide exists between those who believe athletics are integral for the success of the university and those who believe athletics and higher education make strange, and even harmful, bedfellows.

Is the Current Athletics Funding Model Sustainable?

Many have asked whether the current athletics model is sustainable. In short, probably not. However, universities and athletic departments are keeping with the status quo through many strategies, the majority of which fall under the umbrella of corporatization. Corporate sponsorship of every piece of a sporting event is the norm and increasingly an expected part of the college athletics experience. In perhaps the most extreme example, universities are even sponsoring college football postseason bowl games. In 2014, the University of Nebraska and the University of Southern California participated in The National University Holiday Bowl.

As we highlight throughout this text, numerous consequences can potentially result from corporatizing higher education and intercollegiate athletics. As Zimbalist (1999) highlighted, many of the scandals that have rocked intercollegiate athletics were indirect, and sometimes direct, results of a focus on commercialism and profit maximization of amateur athletics. For example, in their discussion of the sexual abuse scandal involving Jerry Sandusky, Bass and Newman (2013) argued the Pennsylvania State University football program, and head coach Joe Paterno, had become "too big to fail." The success of the Nittany Lion football team was so important to the success of the university that it "provided impetus for, if not determined individual action to, the cover up of the Sandusky scandal" (p. 34).

Chapter Summaries

To begin, we provide an extensive overview of the National Collegiate Athletic Association (NCAA). In the second chapter, we highlight the numerous funding mechanisms athletic department administrators use to compete in the high-stakes arena of NCAA Division I intercollegiate athletics. In the third chapter, we examine the ever-increasing corporatization of higher education and the role that intercollegiate athletics, and the funding of intercollegiate athletics, plays in this ongoing process. Finally, we use the concluding chapter to highlight many of the issues intercollegiate athletics is facing and the ways in which those could influence the relationship between higher education and athletics in the coming years. In short, the overarching aim of this text is to analyze, and often critique, the common discourses used when both supporting and decrying the value of athletics to higher education institutions.

Foreword

Jordan R. Bass, Claire C. Schaeperkoetter, and Kyle S. Bunds's monograph, *The "Front Porch": Examining the Increasing Interconnection of University and Athletic Department Funding*, provides an in-depth description and analysis of key financial issues underlying big-time college sports in Division I institutions. The monograph does a great job of explaining the connection between university and athletic department funding by discussing the history of intercollegiate athletics and the NCAA, funding issues pertinent to the role of athletics in higher education, and considerations about the future of athletics in higher education. It offers a critical look at big-time athletics, helping readers, researchers, and practitioners to conceptualize the issues facing intercollegiate athletics today. It addresses important questions about where the funding for athletics comes from, what the potential problems are, and what the future might hold.

I found this monograph particularly compelling for a number of reasons. First, I found the monograph interesting from a personal perspective. I have always been an athlete—though never a particularly good one. I was a downhill ski racer when I was a child, I ran cross-country and track in high school, and I was a rower in college. None of my athletic endeavors were ever good enough to earn me a college scholarship or any particular accolade. My level of skill placed me as a "participant" more than as a top-notch athlete. When I got to college, I continued my love of sports as an avid fan of both the football and basketball teams (men's and women's). I continue to follow both sports—though admittedly I watch more basketball than football (likely a product of where I work). Despite my lifelong love of sports, it wasn't until I was in graduate school that it occurred to me that college and university athletics was not what it seemed to be. I had bought into the "scholar–athlete" ideal and had never been exposed to the idea that athletics was more "big business" than it was an integral part of the mission of the institution. Of course, I had heard of various athletic scandals and was aware that athletics was an expensive endeavor, but I didn't know enough about the enterprise to even ask the right questions. It was in a graduate school class in higher education finance that I became aware of the potential "issues" surrounding big-time college athletics. These prior and current experiences with athletics, coupled with my naïve level of fandom, have made me a sucker for books about college athletics. In fact, every summer I take my pick of the many exposés out there on the topic—from *The System: The Glory and Scandal of Big-Time College Football* by Benedict and Keteyian to *Pay for Play* by Ronald Smith to *Cheated: The UNC Scandal* by Jay Smith and Mary Willingham. There is no shortage of these volumes. This monograph joins these others in illuminating the contradictions that exist between what we hope is the case regarding intercollegiate athletics and what appears to be the reality.

Wearing my professor hat, I see the value in this monograph as well. Many of my students have an interest in intercollegiate athletics—either following it as fans or working with student–athletes. My graduate students hold the same naivety that I carried about athletics. I anticipate this being a popular read among my students and see it as a primer on the topic. The monograph, though not particularly theoretical, provides a solid example of how primary and secondary sources illuminate what is happening in big-time athletics. It is also useful to those in the field and on the front lines of athletics reform. Indeed, this monograph is written for anyone interested in any level of athletics—from fans, to student service providers, to scholars, and to the general public. In summing up the contribution of this work, I would say that it is a thoughtful, timely exploration of where the money to fund higher education comes from and why reform is inevitable, but difficult to enact. It does this in a way that is clear, readable, and comprehensive.

The ASHE Higher Education Report Series has not published much on athletics in a while, although we do have some volumes that address related issues. Recently, for example, the series published two relevant monographs:

Jeffrey Alstete's (2014) monograph on *Revenue Generation Strategies* talks about many of the financial pressures faced by institutions of higher education, and Pauline Reynolds's (2014) monograph, *Representing "U": Popular Culture, Media, and Higher Education*, discusses the role of intercollegiate athletics as it overlaps with popular culture. In 2005, the series published a relevant monograph, *Who Calls the Shots: Sports and University Leadership, Culture and Decision Making*, by Suzanne Estler and Laurie Nelson. We seek further explorations on this topic, as there is a large audience hungry for deep discussions in this particular area.

Of note about this volume is that it is exceedingly readable. The authors present their argument not just by providing numbers, but also by presenting stories. It is clear that the authors bring a level of knowledge to this topic that goes beyond the anecdotal. Of all the things I learned by reading this monograph, the thing that stands out to me is that college athletics, for all its flaws, brings communities and institutions together toward a common cause—to win. This common goal might explain why many people, myself included, remain steadfast fans even though we know that the system is flawed, broken, and potentially going to either self-destruct under its own weight or bring the institutions down with them. This is an easy read for anyone interested in athletics, in funding issues, in organizational governance, in politics, and in leadership. I am pleased to present this monograph as part of our series and believe it makes an important contribution to the field.

Lisa E. Wolf-Wendel
Kelly Ward
Series Editors

Published online in Wiley Online Library
(wileyonlinelibrary.com) • DOI: 10.1002/aehe.20023

A History of Intercollegiate Athletics and the NCAA

S HULMAN AND BOWEN (2001) SURMISED intercollegiate athletic departments make higher education institutions more visible to the public at large, playing a major role in the way institutions communicate with prospective students, parents, alumni, and society. In being a major source of external communication, athletic departments serve as a visible "front porch" for the university as a whole. In his acceptance speech for the 2012 International Brand Master Award presented by the Educational Marketing Group (EMG), Texas A&M Vice President Jason Cook explained how he reinvented the Texas A&M brand by unifying the athletics brand with the university and using sport as the "front porch":

> Our brand was not widely known across the country and the institution was perceived much like it was in the 1970s: a regional, all-male military institution, not the thriving, top-20 research university that it is today. Recognizing that athletics is the "front porch" of a university providing an opportunity to reach millions of people each Saturday in the fall I worked directly with the University's President and Board of Regents to initiate a focused plan in 2011 that would increase the visibility of the Texas A&M brand across the country. This effort culminated with Texas A&M leaving the Big 12 Conference for the Southeastern Conference on July 1, 2012 . . . our plan had three

primary objectives: increase the exposure for our student-athletes and coaches, as well as for our world-class faculty and their research; create new revenue streams in the form of TV payouts, licensing, sponsorships, philanthropy and ticket sales; and provide long-term stability for the Texas A&M brand in a period of significant athletic conference upheaval. The SEC is widely recognized as the nation's top athletic conference, and through its extensive media partnerships with ESPN and CBS, the national exposure generated by the league is unparalleled… Today, because of these efforts, Texas A&M is widely recognized as one of the hottest college brands in the country. (Stephenson, 2013, para. 9)

As another example, think of a major university for which you have minimal familiarity. What is the first image or phrase that comes to mind? Rock Chalk Jayhawk (University of Kansas)? Roll Tide (University of Alabama)? The blue turf at Boise State University? Mike Krzyweski (Duke University)? These are all illustrations of athletics symbols, traditions, and individuals for which major colleges and universities are known nationally and internationally. Thus, in this text, we explore the increasingly entangled relationship between the university and athletic department in this age of big-time college sports. We specifically focus on the many methods in which athletics relies on the university for funding, and in turn the ways in which the university uses these very visible athletic departments to enhance their brand and, ultimately, increase their bottom line through increased enrollment, donations, and similar strategies. The overarching goal of this monograph is to highlight the impact and consequences of the financial and cultural relationships that exist between universities and athletic departments at the NCAA Division I level. We begin with a discussion of the history of the NCAA to set the context for this discussion.

History of the NCAA

The debate on whether National Collegiate Athletic Association student-athletes should be classified as amateurs or employees of their respective universities has reached a fever pitch in recent months both with the Ed O'Bannon federal antitrust trial against the NCAA (Eder & Strauss, 2014) and with Northwestern University's men's football team attempting to unionize in order to receive the workplace rights delineated in the National Labor Relations Act (Resnikoff, 2014). Despite the current groundswell for dramatic changes in the NCAA Division I model, the century-old history of the NCAA indicates that uncertainty and proposed reform have actually been part of the NCAA since its inception (Clotfelter, 2011; Duderstadt, 2009; Zimbalist, 1999). The early stages of the NCAA, restructuring of NCAA divisions, Title IX, and television contracts all point to the notion of changes in the NCAA fueled by financial and legislative motives.

In order to understand the rationale for the original development of the NCAA, it is important to understand the beginnings of athletic activities in collegiate settings in the mid-1800s. In its most grassroots form, collegiate athletics started because of the growing popularity of student-organized athletic activities between students within the insular setting of individual campus environments (Hums & MacLean, 2004). Interest eventually developed to have organized competitions *between* different colleges and universities, and the first intercollegiate athletics competition was a student-organized rowing competition between Yale and Harvard in 1852 (Hums & MacLean, 2004; Weight & Zullo, 2015). Perhaps foreshadowing the eventual corporatization of college athletics, this first intercollegiate athletics competition had its own exclusive sponsorship as the Boston, Concord & Montreal Railroad Company was the official transportation sponsor of the competition (Hums & MacLean, 2004).

Over the next 20 years, this idea of athletic competitions between different colleges and universities continued to expand with the growth of rowing competitions and the start of intercollegiate baseball and football competitions (Hums & MacLean, 2004). As early as the latter part of the 1800s, university administrators voiced concerns about this rapid growth of intercollegiate athletics (Hums & MacLean, 2004; Weight & Zullo, 2015). Specifically, some administrators were worried about the direction of intercollegiate football and its growing influence in the academic setting of college campuses (Hums & MacLean, 2004).

In line with the initial development of intercollegiate athletic competitions, contests continued to be organized by students until the late 1800s. At this point, another larger faction of university administrators began to see the merits of supporting intercollegiate athletics—increased alumni support, branding, and student applications—and pushed for control over the governance and operation of intercollegiate athletic competition at their respective institutions (Hums & MacLean, 2004). As a precursor to the Big Ten Conference, university officials met in Chicago on January 11, 1895, to develop parameters for eligibility, participation, scheduling, equipment, and funding (Hums & MacLean, 2004).

As the popularity of football exploded in the late 1800s, there were a frightening number of serious injuries in intercollegiate football (Duderstadt, 2009; Hums & MacLean, 2004; Wiggins, 1995). In 1905 alone, 18 collegiate players died as a result of on-field injuries and more than 140 were seriously injured (Hums & MacLean, 2004). In response to these events, President Theodore Roosevelt called an emergency meeting at the White House with university administrators from Harvard, Yale, and Princeton to discuss these alarming safety issues with intercollegiate football.

President Roosevelt urged university leaders at Harvard, Yale, and Princeton to develop an organization to bring some structure and integrity into intercollegiate athletics (Duderstadt, 2009; Wiggins, 1995). Another meeting to address similar concerns about football safety took place in December 1905 when the chancellor of New York University (NYU) invited members from 13 other institutions to New York City. Although this meeting at NYU and President Roosevelt's meeting at the White House were called to address football safety issues, it became apparent that a larger group of university administrators shared similar concerns about the safety of college football and also about the governance—or lack thereof—of intercollegiate athletics in the United States (Hums & MacLean, 2004).

In collaboration with the ideas of President Roosevelt and those at the meeting at NYU, 62 members formed the Intercollegiate Athletic Association of the United States (IAAUS) in March 1906 (Duderstadt, 2009; Weight & Zullo, 2015; Wiggins, 1995). The IAAUS would be renamed the National Collegiate Athletic Association (NCAA) in 1910 (Hums & MacLean, 2004).

The 1906 NCAA Constitution laid the groundwork for intercollegiate amateur sport when it asserted: "An amateur sportsman is one who engages in sports for the physical, mental, or social benefits he derives therefrom, and to whom the sport is an avocation. Any college athlete who takes pay for participation in athletics does not meet this definition of amateurism" (Duderstadt, 2009, p. 71).

Even before Roosevelt's directive, however, there were legitimate concerns about the overemphasis of college sports in American society. In his 1893 annual report, Harvard President Charles Eliot declared, "With athletics considered as an end in themselves, pursued either for pecuniary profit or popular applause, a college or university has nothing to do. Neither is it an appropriate function for a college or university to provide periodical entertainment during term-time for multitudes of people who are not students" (as cited in Clotfelter, 2011, p. 10). Despite this unease about the direction of college athletics, the popularity of college athletics, particularly football, continued to soar among students, alumni, and the general population alike after the founding of the NCAA (Duderstadt, 2009). For those potential fans with little direct connection to the university, athletics truly did become the metaphoric front porch for the university; the athletic department was becoming arguably the most visible faction of the university.

As a result of the growing power of athletics in the university setting, football coaches began to have more authority. A specific example at the University of Michigan demonstrates this power shift. In 1906, the same year the NCAA was founded, the Big Ten began to develop and enforce more stringent conference rules. Specifically, it was decided that a coach at a Big Ten institution must be a full-time employee of their institution (Byers & Hammer, 1995). Field Yost, the football coach at the time at the University of Michigan, had external businesses, so he was not a supporter of the new conference role limiting external employment opportunities. Coach Yost said he thought the University of Michigan should leave the Big Ten Conference. Michigan's university president, James Burrill Angell, wanted to remain a member of the Big Ten (Byers & Hammer, 1995). Coach Yost skirted university protocol and pushed for the board of regents at the University of Michigan to call for Michigan to leave the Big Ten. The university regents sided with the coach, and Michigan left the Big Ten conference for 11 years (Byers & Hammer, 1995). Walter Byers, who was elected as the NCAA's first executive director in 1951 (Byers & Hammer, 1995; Hums & MacLean, 2004), said,

> *I believe this showdown was more significant in charting the course of college athletics than the founding of the NCAA that same year… This act of a coach steamrolling his college president had historic significance although the lesson had to be relearned time and again by succeeding generations of college chief executives. (Byers & Hammer, 1995, p. 37)*

Byers's concerns about the power dynamic between athletics personnel and university administrators mimic the sentiments expressed by Weight & Zullo (2015). While detailing the modern-day structure of intercollegiate athletics, they assert that power struggles between university administrators and high-profile coaches (who often make more money than university presidents) continue to demonstrate that oftentimes university administration does not have the final say about athletic department decisions at their university (Weight & Zullo, 2015).

Little more than 20 years after the founding of the NCAA, a 1929 report by the Carnegie Foundation indicated great trepidation over the direction of college football, asserting it was rife with unnecessary commercialization and professionalization to the detriment of both athletic departments and the universities themselves (Duderstadt, 2009; Wiggins, 1995). According to Duderstadt (2009), "the report went on to note that the relationship between intercollegiate athletics and their academic hosts had long been an uneasy one and called for de-emphasis of football" (p. 72). There was no deemphasizing. The popularity of college athletics continued to grow. In fact, the 1920s became the so-called "Golden Age of Sport" and institutions felt pressure from alumni and fans to continue to grow intercollegiate athletics (Wiggins, 1995). Although the Carnegie Report brought to light many concerns about the current state and future direction of intercollegiate athletics, it did not bring drastic changes to the structure of the NCAA (Wiggins, 1995).

Over the next 15 years, the NCAA would continue to add more sports, national championships, and members. Additionally, there were growing concerns about recruiting, financial aid guidelines for student-athletes, and the role of the media (Hums & MacLean, 2004). This, combined with the effect that the end of World War II had on increased enrollment and changing finances in colleges and universities across the country, led to the establishment of a brick-and-mortar office for full-time NCAA personnel in Kansas City. In 1951, Walter Byers was hired as the first executive director for the NCAA (Byers & Hammer, 1995; Hums & MacLean, 2004).

Whereas the NCAA now had a more formalized hierarchical in-house structure with more full-time NCAA personnel, the notions of amateurism and grants-in-aid created a powerful philosophical divide between the northern and southern regions of the United States (Byers & Hammer, 1995). Post–World War II culture in the United States actually served as the impetus for many of these dramatic differences. Many World War II veterans were older, more experienced athletically, and more skilled because of their participation on military-based athletic teams while serving in the military (Byers & Hammer, 1995). Additionally, the commercialization of airline travel in the United States enabled coaches to travel with greater ease to recruit at a national level. In 1948, the NCAA adopted the Sanity Code. This code marked a true effort by the NCAA to establish some specific parameters on the allowable amount of financial aid that could be given to intercollegiate athletes. If the athlete was either in the top 25% of his high school class or maintained a B average in college, he could have his tuition and fees paid for. Essentially, the student would receive a full-ride scholarship based on athletic ability if he met the aforementioned academic standards (Byers & Hammer, 1995).

Colleges and universities in the southern regions of the United States believed the Sanity Code created an unfair advantage for the Big Ten Conference and the Ivy League—conferences that were established and had the financial resources to actually be able to offer prospective athletes such a financial package. Indeed, talented athletes from the south headed to schools in the north that could entice them with a robust financial aid package and a guarantee of admission into their university (Byers & Hammer, 1995). The South wanted to use the grant-in-aid concept—a concept that would rely less on the academic merits of the prospective athlete. Ultimately, the Sanity Code concept was discontinued because the NCAA did not receive the required two-thirds majority vote to expel those who had been in violation of it. Essentially, that left the NCAA with an unenforceable rule. The true grant-in-aid concept was then adopted by more and more colleges as competition in recruiting athletes increased (Byers & Hammer, 1995).

In the book *Unsportsmanlike Conduct: Exploiting College Athletes* (Byers & Hammer, 1995), Byers discusses how he served as a driving force behind the development of the specific term "student-athlete." Byers poignantly acknowledges that the development of this concept has formed the foundation of the pay-for-play debate that rages on today (Byers & Hammer, 1995). Thus, it merits mention that this specific discussion of the development of the student-athlete terminology uses the timeline discussed by Byers himself because he was the most powerful voice behind the development of the definition of student-athlete. Ultimately, the fallout from the Sanity Code and the ensuing popularity of the grant-in-aid concept led to the adoption of the specific term "student-athlete." Byers is credited with the development of this term in an effort to make it so that student-athletes would not be considered employees of the university. Byers knew that if athletes were legally designated as employees, the university would be responsible for covering the prohibitively expensive cost of workers' compensation. He foresaw the extended commercialization efforts of intercollegiate athletics and knew that classifying college athletes as employees could crumble the financial structure of the NCAA itself.

Systemic Changes in College Athletics in the 1970s and 1980s

During the 1970s and 1980s, three systemic, groundbreaking, and relatively simultaneous key movements helped to dramatically change the dynamic of the NCAA: (a) There was a separation of NCAA member schools into different divisions, (b) Title IX radically changed the impetus for NCAA member institutions to increase the inclusion of women's athletic teams, and (c) with the advent of cable television, there was a great opportunity for the NCAA to capitalize on the sport television market. Importantly, all three of these movements are intimately tied together by the distinct motive for the NCAA to increase revenue.

Formation of Three NCAA Divisions

In 1973, the NCAA divided its member institutions into Divisions I, II, and III. The top revenue producers were funneled into Division I, where athletes could receive full athletic scholarships that covered tuition and housing. Division II athletes could receive partial athletic scholarships, and Division III athletes could not receive scholarships based on athletic merit (Yost, 2010). In the late 1990s, there was restructuring within Division I into Division I-A, I-AA, and I-AAA, with revenue generation serving as the primary filtering mechanism (Yost, 2010). Ultimately, NCAA member institutions differentiate themselves across divisions based on funding of athletic programs, scholarships for student-athletes, and fan interest (NCAA, 2014a). On its own website, the NCAA acknowledges the drawing power of football and men's basketball by saying

> *Most Division I institutions … choose to devote more financial resources to support their athletics programs, and many are able to do so because of the large media contracts Division I conferences are able to attract, mostly to showcase the publicly popular sports of football and men's basketball. (para. 3)*

The NCAA Division I membership includes approximately 250 colleges and universities with more than 170,000 Division I student-athletes (NCAA, 2014d). Many athletes receive full or partial athletics scholarships that fully cover tuition and room and board (Yost, 2010). Within the Division I level, there are three subdivisions for football purposes. Football Bowl Subdivision (FBS) schools—what is typically thought of as "big-time" Division I—are eligible to participate in football bowl games. Football Championship Subdivision (FCS) schools participate in an end-of-season 24-team playoff. The third division is made up of Division I schools that do not sponsor football (e.g., St. Louis University, Marquette University; NCAA, 2014d).

Importantly, Division I universities typically have larger athletic department operating budgets than their Division II and Division III counterparts, primarily because of increased fan interest and television rights contracts (NCAA, 2014d). The revenue specifically for the NCAA (and not its member institutions) mostly comes from the television broadcasting contracts for the NCAA Division I men's basketball tournament that takes place during March and April of every year (NCAA, 2014d). Payouts for television broadcasting contracts for football and men's basketball can exceed $25 million annually for some schools (Benedict & Keteyian, 2013).

The Division II membership includes more than 110,000 Division II student-athletes across approximately 300 Division II member institutions (NCAA, 2014a, 2014b). Again, the most salient difference between the Division II model and the other NCAA divisions is the financial scholarship model for student-athletes. Division II athletics follows the partial-scholarship model for its student athletes. Sometimes also called an "equivalency" system, each sport is awarded a number of full scholarships that they are allowed to parcel out to student-athletes. For example, at the Division II level, each football team receives the equivalent of 36 full scholarships that they are allowed to divide up among a squad size that may near 100 student-athletes. In comparison, at the NCAA Division I FBS level, a football team receives 85 full scholarships that may not be divided up; an FBS student-athlete either receives a full athletic scholarship or they receive no athletic scholarship at all (NCAA, 2014b).

The Division II financial operating model provides a cost-effective strategy for NCAA schools to administer an athletics program. Because of lower operating costs than at the Division I level (i.e., lower recruiting and travel expenditures and less expensive facilities and coaches), Division II schools are able to operate without large payouts from television contracts and ticket sales (NCAA, 2014b).

The NCAA Division III level includes 450 member institutions. More than 180,000 student-athletes currently participate in Division III athletics (NCAA, 2014e). The primary distinction between Division III student-athletes and their Division I and Division II counterparts is that they are not allowed to receive athletic scholarships. Relatedly, Division III student-athletes are fully integrated into the general campus community and are primarily focused on academics (NCAA, 2014c, 2014e). These fundamental ideas are conveyed in the Division III Philosophy Statement (NCAA, 2014c):

> *[Division III institutions] shall not award financial aid to any student on the basis of athletics leadership, ability, participation or performance. (para. 4)*

> *[Division III institutions] assure that athletics participants are not treated differently from other members of the student body. (para. 9)*

Title IX

Another major movement during the 1970s and 1980s that drastically altered the trajectory of the NCAA was the inception of Title IX. A provision in the 1972 Education Amendments, it mandated that no person should be excluded from having the opportunity to participate in any educational program receiving federal financial assistance (Shaw, 1995). Under the umbrella of a university structure that receives federal financial assistance, colleges and universities began to fund women's athletic programs, programs that were not necessarily part of the NCAA structure (Sperber, 1990). In the early 1970s, women sport activists started a national organization called the Association of Intercollegiate Athletics for Women (AIAW). In an intentional move to differentiate itself from the NCAA, the AIAW promoted participation and education, in stark contrast to the ever-commercialized NCAA product (Sperber, 1990).

The NCAA did not initially feel threatened by the AIAW, but when the AIAW programs received increased funding from the universities, the NCAA and university athletic directors saw an opportunity to increase revenue. By offering NCAA membership discounts (and all-expenses paid trips to NCAA championships) to institutions that would enroll their AIAW women's programs into the NCAA, universities could align themselves with an athletic association at a drastically discounted rate. In a final crushing blow related to the all-important television contract "the NCAA tied the sale of its men's Final Four to its new women's basketball championship game, guaranteeing a major network for the event and making it more attractive to schools than the AIAW final" (Sperber, 1990). In June 1982, the AIAW folded (Sperber, 1990).

It has been more than 40 years since Congress enacted the federal statute widely known as Title IX. A closer look at the words of Title IX, the historical developments of Title IX, and some of the unintended consequences of Title IX reveal that Title IX is much more complex than just a pat on the back for female athletic participation. It has dramatically altered the structure of college athletics and the role of athletics in the college institution at large.

Statistical changes in the American workforce in the 1960s provided the original impetus for what would eventually become Title IX. The 1960s saw a large increase in the number of women in the workforce, an increase that went hand in hand with an increased number of women in higher education. College applications that placed higher admittance standards on females were the norm. Females testified in front of Congress, claiming that university admission quotas were commonplace. There were also stories of females losing financial aid if they got married while in college (Gavora, 2002). The original intent of Title IX was not to make college athletics a balancing act of gender-based quotas. When Title IX was enacted in 1972, few people thought Title IX would ultimately have its greatest, and most contentiously debated, effects in athletics. The Education Amendments of 1972 were enacted to mirror many of the purer motives behind the Civil Rights Act of 1964—a fundamental right for equality and fairness.

As part of the Education Amendments of 1972, Title IX reads, "No person in the United States shall, on the basis of sex, be excluded from participation in, be denied the benefits of, or be subjected to discrimination under any education program or activity receiving Federal financial assistance" (Shaw, 1995, p. 7). Those familiar with the Civil Rights Act of 1964 will note that much of the language of Title IX is very similar to the Civil Rights Act of 1964. More or less using the wording of the Civil Rights Act as a template, the notion of Title IX started to form in 1970 as part of a special House Subcommittee on Education (Anderson, 2012).

After the enactment of the Educational Amendments of 1972, the Department of Education's Office of Civil Rights (OCR) began to provide specific guidelines about Title IX's effect on intercollegiate athletic programs (Reich, 2003). Throughout this process, it became abundantly clear that the OCR would be the governmental agency taking the lead on Title IX enforcement. Thus, although the specific language of Title IX seems relatively straightforward and well intentioned, its expansion into college athletics has really relied on the OCR's administration of Title IX enforcement as well as judicial decisions in order to tease apart the tangible effects of Title IX on college athletics (Judge, O'Brien, & O'Brien, 1995).

Upon the enactment of Title IX, Congress and athletic administrators saw the road Title IX was heading down and saw the potential negative consequences it could have on revenue-generating college sports. Thus, in the years immediately following the enactment of Title IX, several bills were introduced in Congress to attempt "to stop what some believed was its potential negative impact on revenue-producing sports in collegiate athletics. None of these amendments passed" (Anderson, 2012, p. 4). More than 40 years later, these so-called "negative consequences" of Title IX continue to shape the heated debate that surrounds Title IX.

In response to the bills proposed in Congress in the years immediately following Title IX, Congress passed the Javits Amendment on August 21, 1974. Also known as the Education Amendments of 1974, the Javits Amendment specifically stated the applicability of Title IX to athletic activities. It required the Department of Health, Education, and Welfare to

> *prepare and publish.... proposed regulations implementing the provisions of Title IX of the Education Amendments of 1972 relating to the prohibition of sex discrimination in federally affected education programs which shall include with respect to intercollegiate athletic activities reasonable provisions considering the nature of particular sports. (Anderson, 2012, p. 4)*

The second issue that added to the confusion about the enforcement of Title IX in the 1970s had to do with the OCR's 1979 Policy Interpretation that released the development of the three-pronged test for athletic departments to use to assess Title IX compliance (Judge et al., 1995). The three-pronged test for effective accommodation allows institutions to demonstrate Title IX compliance by:

1. Providing opportunities for participation in intercollegiate sports by gender in approximate proportion to undergraduate enrollment (substantial proportionality);
2. Demonstrating a "history and continuing practice" of expanding opportunities for the underrepresented gender (continued expansion); or
3. Presenting proof that it is "fully and effectively" accommodating the athletic interest of the underrepresented gender (full accommodation) (Stafford, 2004, p. 1470).

To this day, there is still a considerable amount of confusion about the functionality and importance of the three-pronged test. In fact, "substantial proportionality has never been explicitly defined by OCR" (Stafford, 2004, p. 1470) but rather has been taken in practice to mean that the percentage of female athletes must be within five percentage points of the female percentage in the general undergraduate student body. Furthermore, there is confusion about what exactly an institution must do to demonstrate both a "history and continuing practice" of continued expansion and "full accommodation." As a result of this confusion, there has been an inherent tendency to rely on the substantial proportionality test part of the prong test in order to adhere to Title IX compliance. Perhaps telling of both the confusion about Title IX and the resistance to Title IX, "for the 1995–1996 school year, only 29 of the 321 Division I intercollegiate athletic programs achieved substantial proportionality"—a rate of 9.03% (Stafford, 2004, p. 1470).

Such a low percentage should not be surprising, especially if the NCAA's general initial opposition to Title IX is taken into consideration. Thelin (2000) sums up the NCAA's general resistance to Title IX when he outlines the NCAA's efforts:

> From the point of view of university athletic departments and the NCAA, their efforts for equity for women's sports did not begin in 1972, when Title IX was passed into law. First, they opposed

Title IX and testified to Congress against it. Second, even when Ti-
tle IX was passed in 1972 it carried with it two phases that gave
colleges and universities a buffer from regulation. From 1972 to
1975 there was no Congressional enforcement or scrutiny, because
those three years were devoted to federal agencies drafting guide-
lines, holding discussions and meetings, and trying to agree on and
then publish criteria. When guidelines were published in 1975,
the federal government gave colleges and universities a three-year
period in suspense, with institutional reviews being delayed until
1978 at the earliest. (p. 397)

Finally, and arguably most tellingly, the NCAA did not include women's sports in its constitution and bylaws until 1981—a full 9 years after the passage of Title IX at a time when women's programs in the AIAW continued to receive increased funding for their female athletic programs (Sperber, 1990).

The general resistance to Title IX in intercollegiate athletics was not confined to those administrators in NCAA headquarters. In 1979, Southeastern Conference leaders publicly acknowledged that "inflation and the cost of adding sports to the program were major concerns among SEC Athletic Directors" (Thelin, 2000, p. 392). The proposed solution for these athletic directors was to increase fundraising efforts rather than reduce spending. Ironically, in the current age of the so-called Division I arms race, there is more pressure to increase fundraising efforts than there is to tighten the proverbial budgetary belt.

In 1972, the year Title IX was passed, one in nine girls played high school sports (Gavora, 2002). The failure to acknowledge that there was a drastic uptick in female athletic participation certainly does not negate the effects of Title IX, but it does reflect that there was momentum for female athletic participation before Title IX. Thus, it should be noted that perhaps Title IX was not the starting line for female athletic participation but rather a reflection of the momentum of female interest in athletics participation.

Proponents of a male-dominated revenue-driven athletic department mentality frequently fail to point out that colleges and universities had a hard time being financially self-sustaining in traditional spectator sports before Title IX was part of the NCAA Constitution (Thelin, 2000). To accentuate this point, the University of Colorado eliminated men's baseball, swimming, wrestling, and tennis a full year before the NCAA added women's sports as part of its jurisdiction in 1981. Coincidentally or not, fan interest in sports such as baseball, wrestling, tennis, and gymnastics declined *before* Title IX was explicitly part of the NCAA.

Contrary to some of the other men's sports, football had significant fan interest before Title IX, is often the primary sport included in the TV deals that frequently top $100 million, and is the main sport at the center of the Title IX debate. With 85 players on scholarship and a total squad list that usually exceeds 100 players including walk-on athletes, there simply is not a traditional female sport that can keep up with the sheer numbers of male athletes on football teams. Money spent just on recruiting and travel for football teams is absolutely mind-boggling (Salter, 1996). As will be discussed later when detailing many of the unintended consequences of Title IX, two of the primary strategies for athletic departments to attempt to match football numbers with female athletes for Title IX purposes are either to cut other men's programs or to add unpopular, high-number sports like rowing or equestrianism.

Proponents of Title IX point to the bloated numbers on college football teams and recommend decreasing football squad sizes. Football enthusiasts campaign for Title IX exemptions and even separating from the NCAA. History has shown an unwillingness to listen to the other side. Thus, the debate about football and Title IX continues. Doctor Christine Grant, former athletic director at the University of Iowa, advocated for some sort of resolution when she said:

> *Each campus has to sit down and decide what are the purposes of intercollegiate athletics. If the purposes are to bring in money and to provide the largest PR arm for the university, then we have got to be up front and say, this is why we are doing it. If it is not the reason, then we have got to put it in an educational framework that makes sense. At least tell me what is the real purpose of intercollegiate athletics. (Salter, 1996, p. 45)*

The coaches and fans of the nonrevenue men's sports are often caught in the middle. Should they take the stance that football is indirectly to blame for the recent trend of cutting nonrevenue men's sports for Title IX reasons? Or, rather, should the blame be put on Title IX itself for the quota system it has seemingly created? Basic facts continue to demonstrate that, from an operating budget standpoint, women's sports are still significantly behind men's. An internal NCAA study revealed that "men's teams receive 70 percent of athletic scholarship money, 77 percent of the operating budget, and 83 percent of the recruiting money at large Division I-A institutions" (Salter, 1996, p. 53).

The sport of football has created the most difficulty in what has become a delicate numbers balancing act for Title IX compliance. From a historical standpoint, there has been resistance to Title IX from the football community since the birth of Title IX in 1972. With squad sizes that have hovered around 100 athletes, it was clear that drastic changes would have to be made for those schools that had football programs to come close to Title IX compliance. With the popularity of college football taking off, an alarmed Senator John Tower, an ardent football supporter and member of a fan base that worried Title IX would signal the demise of college football, sponsored an amendment that became known as the Tower Amendment. The amendment proposed that revenue-generating sports would not be factored into Title IX calculations. Entered into Congress in 1974, the Tower Amendment was passed in the Senate but was then dropped in a House–Senate conference committee (Sigelman & Wahlbeck, 1999). In the 40 years since the Tower Amendment was rejected, the push for a football exemption from Title IX has continued to be a hot button issue.

Another scenario that has been proposed in order to combat the issues football posed to Title IX compliance efforts is the idea that squad sizes should be reduced. Unsurprisingly, football coaches' associations have been up in arms that this proposal has even been discussed as a viable option. However, the fact is that at many Division I institutions, there are as many football student-athletes as there are female student-athletes across all female teams combined (Sigelman & Wahlbeck, 1999). As previously mentioned, instead of cutting back on football squad sizes, there has been more of a movement to reduce male numbers by cutting men's nonrevenue sports. Sigelman and

Wahlbeck (1999) conducted a statistical research study that looked at what kind of cutbacks it would take to reach Title IX compliance if no women's sports were added and just men's sports were cut. The researchers found that, with football players making up 40% of the male athletes at the median Division I-A school (currently FBS), a Division I FBS school would have to go from 167 male nonfootball male athletes to 41 (Sigelman & Wahlbeck, 1999). Clearly, other options, including football squad size reductions, should continue to be discussed.

Football coaches adamantly argue that squad sizes should not be reduced, noting the already inherent safety concerns of such a violent sport. They point out that fewer players on the team would overexpose athletes to injury. The NCAA headed an Injury Surveillance System summary for the 2000–2001 season that revealed that the "serious injury rate during games in football was 14.1 per 1000 athletic exposures" (Simon, 2005, p. 74) based largely on the assumption that for any given NCAA football game, approximately 60 players participate in the game. Even conservative estimates using information from the Injury Surveillance System summary indicate that football injuries would not increase with reduced roster sizes (Simon, 2005). Although certainly no one on either side of the Title IX debate would want even one player injured per game, the study did reveal that reducing squad sizes would not necessarily result in a huge increase in the safety concerns that college football coaches fear so greatly. Furthermore, from a financial standpoint, there is certainly an incentive to decrease football squad sizes. "If football scholarships were cut to 60, the average college would save approximately $750,000 annually, enough to finance more than two wrestling teams—whose average cost is $330,000 per team" (Simon, 2005, p. 73). Additionally, in the National Football League (NFL), teams have a roster cap of 52 players, with a maximum of 45 that can play in any given NFL game (Simon, 2005).

There have been other strategies more commonly put in place to meet the Title IX "substantial proportionality" standards—namely adding less popular women's sports with large squad sizes. Recognizing that many schools would need to add women's sports in order to move toward Title IX compliance, the NCAA recommended that schools added "emerging sports" to create more possibilities for females to join intercollegiate athletic teams. Suggested team sports were crew (rowing), ice hockey, handball, water polo, and synchronized swimming. Suggested individual sports were archery, badminton, bowling, and squash (Reich, 2003). Few would argue that any of these sports are widely popular across the United States.

Sadly, albeit somewhat humorously, there have been numerous examples of schools going to extreme lengths to add women's sports that from a geographic and popularity standpoint make very little sense to add. Arizona State University, a school that is unsurprisingly in the desert, had to flood a valley so that its newly created women's crew program could have a place to practice. The Ohio State University placed ads in the student newspaper reading "Tall athletic women wanted. No experience necessary" (Reich, 2003, p. 531).

Much of the consternation about Title IX has to do not only with how to stay out of the red financially but also with confusion over how Title IX compliance is even measured and enforced. In 1979, the OCR issued a Policy Interpretation to provide enforcement instructions to athletic departments on three issues they deemed were directly tied to Title IX: scholarships, benefits and opportunities, and effective accommodation of student interests and abilities (Jurewitz, 2000). Eventually known as the three-part test to measure substantial proportionality, continued expansion, and full accommodation, it has received plenty of criticism from all sides of the Title IX debate for several reasons (Stafford, 2004).

First, neither Congress nor the president ever approved the policy interpretation, yet it is the primary framework that is used to measure Title IX compliance. Second, the substantial proportionality prong does not actually specify if there is any percentage point leeway when it comes to matching student-athlete gender percentages with gender percentages for that undergraduate institution as a whole (Porto, 1996). The second prong, continued expansion, does not specify how many women's teams need to be added in a specified time frame in order to satisfy the compliance standard. Also, with budgetary constraints putting more and more pressure on athletic directors, there have been limited examples of athletic departments spending the money to add teams to satisfy the second prong. With the third prong, there has been criticism on how a school would prove that females are being "effectively accommodated" (Porto, 1996). As a consequence of some of the concerns mentioned with satisfying the second prong—namely the expenses associated with adding teams—there really are not many ways to prove effective accommodation if continued expansion has not been taking place. As such, there are confusion and criticism about each of the three prongs. However, the first prong, substantial proportionality, seems to provide the most tangible method to measure Title IX compliance. Thus, most schools attempt to use the substantial proportionality prong to satisfy Title IX regulations (Sigelman & Wahlbeck, 1999).

Consequently, a very significant portion of Title IX compliance is centered on what substantial proportionality really means and whether or not it is an appropriate measure for the intent of Title IX. Critics say it either does not accurately measure the athletic interests of females or it leads to a numbers game that has created serious concerns about reverse affirmative action (Sigelman & Wahlbeck, 1999). They say formulas and percentages cannot correctly enforce the original intent of Title IX (Jurewitz, 2000). Jurewitz summed up the notion that the three-prong test does not accurately reflect the original intent of Title IX when he says:

> Congress never intended Title IX to allocate half of all spaces in theatre or literature classes for men, or half of all spaces in science and math classes for women. Congress merely intended for students of each sex, free from discrimination, to select the education programs in which they wished to participate. (p. 351)

Some pundits argue that even though Title IX has received the most publicity as it relates to athletics, it continues to tap into the central motive that drove Title IX in the first place—educational equality. Salter (1996) addressed this notion of Title IX and educational equality when he says:

> Sports are a microcosm of society in that many, if not all, of the attributes required to compete and be successful in the athletic arena are prerequisites for basic survival. Whether it is in business, law, or medicine, people need the skills to work as a team, to be able to function effectively under pressure, and to exhibit simpler traits like responsibility and discipline. Are these

characteristics not as important for our daughters to learn as they are for our sons? (p. 9)

Title IX has often received the majority of the blame for the forced creation of women's sports teams like rowing and equestrian that do not generate much participatory interest and for the elimination of nonrevenue men's teams. However, the Commission on Opportunities in Athletics succinctly stated it believes it is unfair to place all the blame on Title IX when athletic teams are cut from an institution's NCAA offerings. There is no mandate that men's teams be cut. There are other opportunities for the reallocation of resources. The commission's most understated, yet possibly most important, stance was, "The Commission found that it is extremely difficult to obtain a set of data that is accepted by all parties" (Simon, 2005, p. 13). It appears there are no clear-cut answers to the concern and confusion that drives Title IX debate. Perhaps Title IX is best summarized in Brad Reich's (2003) piece that says

Title IX is a regime which has, directly and indirectly, often by fits and starts, and without ever being a model of theoretical elegance of coherence, helped bring about a world in which more and more women and girls share in a set of valuable experiences that were almost the exclusive province of men and boys. (p. 532)

Television Broadcasting Contracts

After the epic 1979 NCAA men's basketball championship game between Larry Bird's Indiana State Sycamores and Magic Johnson's Michigan State Spartans, the NCAA increased its television rights deal with CBS. More important, a true competitor entered the market. The NCAA also struck a deal with the newly formed ESPN to broadcast all men's tournament games that were not televised by CBS (Duderstadt, 2009). Television companies sought out college broadcasting rights because production costs were inherently low. College basketball, along with college football, became both commercial and national products (Duderstadt, 2009). The national interest generated by the stories of Bird and Johnson, combined with the inception of ESPN, created a situation in which the NCAA held significant negotiating power with television companies.

For the first part of the 1980s, the NCAA received between $30 million and $40 million annually combined between CBS and ESPN for television rights for the NCAA tournament. To capitalize on the market opportunity in 1985, the NCAA expanded "March Madness" to a tournament that would include 64 teams and would last 3 weeks (Prisbell & Yanda, 2010). In 1989, CBS and the NCAA agreed to an exclusive broadcasting deal for the NCAA tournament for $1 billion for the next 7 years (Duderstadt, 2009). In 2010, the NCAA reached a 14-year partnered deal with CBS and Turner Sports for $10.8 billion (O'Toole, 2010). The crux of all of these exclusive March Madness television deals is that the NCAA itself, and not its member schools, is receiving the majority of the payout.

During this same time, the NCAA lost its monopoly over college football telecasts as conferences negotiated independently with different broadcasting companies (Sperber, 2000). Although the NCAA itself did not directly receive money from these football broadcasting contracts, the NCAA did regulate the sponsorship deals and payouts for football bowl games. As such, many athletic departments actually lost money when they participated in bowl games (Sperber, 2000).

Although Dave Brandon recently resigned as the athletic director at the University of Michigan, his thoughts conveyed in *The System* reveal that he knew his job security hinged on the success of the Michigan football team. Brandon said, "Michigan athletics cannot be successful if Michigan football does not lead our success, because the revenue it creates is what we live off of" (Benedict & Keteyian, 2013, p. 45). Brandon correctly noted that Division I athletic departments live and die by the financial revenue generated by football, and to a lesser extent, men's basketball. Although ticket sales and booster donations can generate millions of dollars in revenue for college athletic departments, football television contracts often form the primary revenue source for Power Five conferences in college athletics (Benedict & Keteyian, 2013).

Benedict and Keteyian (2013) further posit that "nowhere [is] ESPN's ubiquitous investment in live-event programming more complete or controlling than college football" (p. 371). Additionally, in the Power Five conferences alone, ESPN committed more than $10 billion to long-term broadcasting rights contracts. ESPN does indeed control much of the narrative because of its broadcasting rights for so many regular season games, the College Football Playoff, and 33 of the 35 bowl games that occurred at the conclusion of the 2013 regular season. ESPN and its associated platforms (ABC, ESPN, ESPN2, ESPNU, etc.) aired more than 450 college football games during the 2012 season (Benedict & Keteyian, 2013).

Conclusion

Each NCAA Division I member institution has a faculty athletics representative (FAR) who serves as a liaison between the athletic department and university officials. In a generalized sense, university officials are aware of the revenues and operating expenses of university athletic department. Whereas some universities are housed under the university umbrella, other athletic departments function separately from the university as an auxiliary entity (Clotfelter, 2011; Thelin, 1996). Because of an athletic department's inherent reliance on outside entities such as corporate sponsors, ticket sale revenues, and television broadcast payouts from its athletic conference, athletic departments function like a business more than almost any other university unit (Clotfelter, 2011). Athletic department budgets often are approximately the same as campus professional schools such as engineering, law, or medicine (Thelin, 1996). In instances in which athletic department financial revenues do not meet operating expenses, athletic departments receive subsidies from the university (Clotfelter, 2011).

As the NCAA has grown into a billion-dollar industry, university faculty members have been keenly aware of some of the hotly debated athletic funding issues (Thelin, 1996). Through the American Association of University Professors (AAUP), faculty members were a part of NCAA restructuring debates in the 1980s and 1990s. The AAUP even has publications titled "The Commercialization of College Sports," "Reforming College Sports: How? When? Ever?," and "A Report of the Special Committee on Athletics" (Thelin, 1996).

Since the launch of the NCAA, there has been continual debate about the efficacy and integrity of the NCAA model. Over 100 years ago, there were concerns about player safety, the educational-athletic balance of collegiate athletes, overcommercialization, and funding debates that still rage on today. Whether it was Teddy Roosevelt promoting the amateur model, CBS signing billion-dollar television rights contracts with the NCAA, or student-athletes wanting to be classified as employees of their respective universities, what sparked debate and proposed change has almost always been commercialization and athletic department funding.

In the following three chapters we detail this increasing subsidization of intercollegiate athletics, the prominent corporate influence in higher education, and emerging problems on the horizon that could further complicate the higher education–athletics relationship. In the next chapter, we set the stage for this conversation by highlighting just how dire, and likely unsustainable, the current funding model is for NCAA Division I intercollegiate athletics.

The NCAA Division I Athletic Funding Crisis

U NDERSTANDING THE TRAJECTORY AND SCOPE of the history of the NCAA provides the necessary background with which to explore the athletic funding crisis that has seemingly reached an apex in the current era of intercollegiate athletics. Although intercollegiate athletics started from the humble beginnings of student-organized athletic activities in the mid-1800s (Hums & MacLean, 2004), it functions today as a multibillion dollar industry bolstered in part by billion-dollar television broadcasting rights contracts (O'Toole, 2010) and exclusive million-dollar corporate sponsorships with apparel companies (Giroux, 2007). Such astronomical monetary values flowing into many athletic departments around the country could lead many sport consumers to believe that athletic departments are flush with money. However, as we detail later in this chapter, sport consumers need not be fooled; budgetary funding issues loom large over most athletic departments in NCAA Division I athletics (Sander, 2011).

Further delving into these budgetary issues also illustrates the clairvoyance of the 1929 Carnegie Foundation Report that voiced concern over the seeming overcommercialization of college athletics (Duderstadt, 2009). The very separation of the NCAA into three separate divisions (Divisions I, II, and III) in 1973 was itself prompted by the revenue-generating priorities of NCAA member institutions (Yost, 2010). Additionally, the inception and repercussions of Title IX in the 1970s and 1980s told yet another story of NCAA member institutions' strategies to drive up revenue while also inherently dealing with the legal ramifications of Title IX noncompliance (Sperber, 1990). The sport of football importantly weaves a thread through the separation of the NCAA into three divisions (Yost, 2010), the rapid monetary increase in television broadcasting rights contracts (O'Toole, 2010), and the ongoing issues with roster sizes in regard to Title IX compliance (Sigelman & Wahlbeck, 1999). That is, although football often serves as the primary revenue-generating sport in NCAA Division I athletics, it also often creates large amounts of consternation as athletic department officials delicately try to balance the budget and adhere to NCAA bylaws and legislation in regard to Title IX.

This monograph progresses by delving into an in-depth discussion of the varying important contributors to the athletic funding crisis that serves as arguably the most prominent issue facing collegiate athletics today. Specifically, delineating case study examples of funding issues, outlining the relevance of student fees and tuition allocations, and dissecting the sometimes tenuous relationship between the university itself and the athletic department all demonstrate the need for a greater understanding of the complexities of athletic department funding issues in NCAA Division I athletics. Athletic departments strategize to attempt to close the gap between revenues and (ever-expanding) expenses by relying both on athletic department fundraising efforts and on subsidies from the university at large. Importantly, we also showcase how this athletic department funding gap is not solely limited to non-name-brand athletic departments. These funding issues face many flagship universities as well.

All of these issues provide support for the notion that the relationship between the athletic department and the university—the relationship between the "front porch" and the house itself—is becoming increasingly complicated. Examples vary on whether university administrators want a more prominent athletic department or whether they wish the university would just cut its proverbial losses and invest more heavily in other factions of the university. Ultimately, the idea of the existence of an athletic funding crisis is not necessarily new to the college athletics. As detailed earlier, there have been concerns about commercialization and funding in college athletics for at least a century.

However, evidence indicates that we may have reached a breaking point in regard to divergent priorities of athletic department and university officials.

"You've Got to Keep Up With the Joneses"

When Hurricane Katrina hit the U.S. Gulf Coast in 2005, it caused over $81 billion in damage (Weather Channel, 2009) and destroyed infrastructure through the region, including much of the campus of the University of New Orleans (UNO). In the 3 years that followed the disaster, enrollment at the Division I school decreased by more than 7,000 students (Weaver, 2011). As a consequence, in 2009 university administrators announced the school would be moving from Division I to Division III, a smaller division with lower operating costs where athletic scholarships are not offered.

Chancellor Tim Ryan stated the reasons for the move were twofold: (a) deep state budget cuts necessitated the university to eliminate an annual $2 million subsidy to the athletic department and (b) the loss of 7,000 students hindered the ability of the athletic department to collect sufficient athletics fees from the general student population. Weaver (2011) noted the school was publicly condemned for failing to find a way to survive at the Division I level, even when the athletics department was drowning in expenses that could not be covered alone by the revenues generated within the athletic department. UNO athletics operated at an average annual deficit of $1.2 to $1.5 million since Hurricane Katrina (Wieberg, 2010). Ryan stated the school simply could not afford to remain competitive at the Division I level: "You've got to keep up with the Joneses. Everybody wants to build better facilities. They spend more money on coaching" (quoted in Wieberg, 2010, para. 4). Even with these financial realities, the university ultimately decided to remain in Division I under the auspices of increasing enrollment.

A further review of the state of intercollegiate athletics illustrates that the University of New Orleans was not alone in its reliance on university subsidies and student fees to support the athletic department. Although Hurricane Katrina might have served as a catalyst for rectifying long-term failures in athletic funding practices at the University of New Orleans, we do not need a

TABLE 1
Percentage of Tuition That Goes to Athletic Department in 2010–2011

School	In-State Tuition	Athletic Fee Amount	Athletic Fee %
Norfolk State	6,227.00	1,440.60	23.1
Longwood	9,855.00	2,022.00	20.5
Old Dominion	7,708.00	1,133.01	14.7
James Madison	7,860.00	1,114.00	14.2
Radford	7,694.00	1,077.00	14.0
UNC-Asheville	4,772.10	620.00	13.0
Cal St. Bakersfield	5,314.00	672.00	12.6
Coppin State	5,382.00	679.00	12.6
William and Mary	12,188.00	1,422.00	11.7
North Carolina A&T	4,593.00	532.00	11.6
East Carolina	4,797.00	526.00	11.0
VMI	12,328.00	1,362.00	11.0
Appalachian St.	5,284.74	569.00	10.8
Western Carolina	5,998.80	617.00	10.3
Florida Atlantic	4,924.10	493.50	10.0
UNC-Wilmington	5,415.90	541.25	10.0
Towson	7,656.00	767.00	10.0

Source: Data generated from *USA Today chart: Analyzing the percentage of tuition that goes to athletics for the 2010–2011 school year in public universities in the United States*, http://sports.usatoday.com/ncaa/finances/

catastrophic disaster elsewhere to see that many schools have yet to fully deal with the untenable and unsustainable funding models that now hold sway over intercollegiate athletics in the United States. As is evidenced in Table 1, a limited number of Division I athletic departments generate enough revenue to fully cover their expenses. Departments often rely heavily on student fees and tuition reallocations to operate.

The ever-present gap between revenues and expenses in college athletics further prioritizes fundraising efforts. The median athletic department deficit at the Division I level was $11.6 million in 2010, the same as in 2009 (Sander, 2011). According to a *USA Today* investigation, seven NCAA Division I public universities logged more than $100 million in athletic expenses during the 2011 school year (*USA Today*, 2012). All seven of these schools (University of Texas, Ohio State University, the University of Michigan, the University of Florida, the University of Alabama, Pennsylvania State University, and Auburn University) received a less than 5% subsidy from allocated sources, partially because they were all able to generate an average of $31 million in outside contributions. An unnamed author for the *USA Today* defined these types of contributions as:

> *amounts received directly from individuals, corporations, associations, foundations, clubs or other organizations by the donor for the operation of the athletics program. Report amounts paid in excess of a ticket's value. Contributions include cash, marketable securities and in-kind contributions such as dealer-provided cars, apparel and drink products for team and staff use. Also includes revenue from preferential seating. (2012, para. 14)*

Here, as in other discussions around issues of funding for intercollegiate athletics, "allocated sources" is an encompassing term used to describe student fees, institutional support, and money from the state that athletic departments receive as a subsidy to help offset their expenses.

On the other end of the expenditure spectrum, four Division I schools (Coppin State, Mississippi Valley State, North Carolina Asheville, & Maryland-Eastern Shore) had under $5 million in expenses in 2011. However, all four schools represented at least 50% of their "revenue" as coming from allocated sources. Moreover, Coppin State and Maryland-Eastern Shore required subsidization of more than 80% from allocated sources to keep the departments operational. The four schools generated a combined $410,083 in contributions during 2011, or 2% of their annual expenses. In contrast, the seven schools that spent more than $100 million generated $222,149,705 in contributions, or 28% of their annual expenses. The gap in expenses between the groups is not surprising, as the top seven schools have more sports, athletes, and coaches to support than the latter four schools. Additionally, the gap in the amount of money raised between the two groups is not overly surprising considering the benefits received (e.g., coveted tickets, parking spots, access) for contributions and popularity and visibility of schools in the former group. For example, the University of Texas received more than $42 million in rights and licensing fees in 2011. However, the difference in the two groups in the percentage of expenses that is covered by booster contributions is certainly worth further consideration, especially considering the current economic climate in higher education. In short, student fees and state funds are propping up the four schools that have under $5 million in expenses, although these schools generate very little revenue within the department and collect minimal amounts of contributions.

This cash flow problem is certainly not just limited to schools with smaller athletics programs. The University of California-Berkeley, a prestigious Pacific-12 conference school, is a prime example of an athletic department under a financial crunch. In 2010, Cal-Berkeley announced it was cutting five programs (baseball, men's rugby, men's and women's gymnastics, and women's lacrosse) because the teams were losing money and being subsidized through allocations while academic departments were being downsized or eliminated (Drape, 2010). The move was expected to save the university more than $4 million. However, the program cuts did not come close to making Cal-Berkeley a self-sustaining program. In 2011, a year after the cuts, the athletic department received more than $10 million in allocations from the students, university, and state. Chancellor Robert J. Birgeneau said the cuts would reduce costs and lower institutional support to "reasonable levels" (Public Affairs, 2010). Funding from the university did decrease by $1.6 million in 2011. However, contributions also decreased by more than $2 million from 2010 to 2011, essentially leaving Cal-Berkeley in the same predicament they were in before. This all came at a time when state funding for the Cal-Berkeley campus was cut by upwards of $80 million (Freedberg, 2011).

A group appropriately titled "Save Cal Sports" led a massive fundraising campaign that generated enough funds to reinstate all five sports. For each sport to continue, boosters were required to raise enough money to make the sport sustainable for the next 7 to 10 years. In total, the ad hoc boosters department raised more than $25 million. However, Zennie Abraham (2011) of the *San Francisco Chronicle* speculated the athletic department might have been secretly rooting for the sports to remain cut to ensure the improved sustainability of the other 24 athletic teams, an inordinate amount of programs that is rivaled by only a few schools. Abraham noted the university athletic website did not have any mentions of the fundraising efforts or any links to the donation pages. A combination of low ticket sales for the football and men's basketball teams coupled with supporting 29 varsity sports made it nearly impossible for Cal-Berkeley to continue operating without state assistance.

Cal-Berkeley, of course, is not the only school facing a budget shortfall. Joe Drape (2010) of *The New York Times* noted that Football Bowl Subdivision athletic departments increased their spending by more than 10% from 2008 to 2009 while receiving an additional 28% in allocations from the university. Drape noted the increase in expenses and allocations coincided with universities nationwide making "painful" cuts to their academic programs. Until recently, this trend of funding athletics with public funds has gone unchecked.

Student Fees, Tuition Reallocation, and Athletic Department Funding

Student fee subsidization of athletics and ancillary activities is certainly nothing new. Universities have charged students mandatory fees that are added onto tuition costs to cover anything from technology costs to health services as far back as 1875 (Foundation for Individual Rights in Education, 2012) when the University of Wisconsin charged students for heating and lighting the university. During the 2008–2009 school year, students nationwide were charged more than $795 million in student fees to subsidize athletic departments at 222 Division I public schools. Berkowitz, Upton, McCarthy, and Gillum (2010) noted that even when they accounted for inflation, the cumulative fee amount increased an astonishing 18% since 2005. In Table 1, the 17 schools whose students paid more than 10% of their base in-state tuition in athletic fees during the 2010–2011 school year are listed.

Berkowitz et al. (2010) explained how public schools in the state of Virginia use student athletic fees as a loophole to avoid a state law banning the use of tuition/public money to fund athletics. In turn, six schools in the state charged more than $1,000 per student to support the athletic department during the 2008–2009 school year. These fees were often buried within financial jargon and not specifically disclosed on billing statements.

Of the 17 schools listed in Table 1, 15 did not disclose the athletics fee each student pays on billing statements or in university promotional materials. Berkowitz et al. (2010) quoted a spokesman from Virginia Military Institute as stating the institution buries its athletics fee in the budget where "[nobody] would go look for it." Similarly, Towson University in Maryland began publishing the athletics fee on its website only after it was questioned about its compliance with higher education transparency laws.

Perhaps even more problematic, scholars argued less affluent students were most affected by athletic student fees. In a paper from the Center for College Affordability and Productivity, Denhart and Vedder (2010) stated athletic department subsidies were "highly regressive, hitting the poor more than the rich" (p. 4). They defined "poor" in two contexts: (a) universities that were short on institutional resources and should not be funding anything other than academics and (b) students who came from lower income backgrounds compared to students at other universities. Denhart and Vedder (2010) used the percentage of the students receiving Pell grants and total core university expenditures to determine the wealth of the students and overall institution. They discovered that teams in the conferences with the highest wealth based on their classification received the lowest amount of subsidies. They argued that this reallocation of funds, in effect, made athletic subsidizes a regressive tax. They compared two schools within 50 miles of each other, the University of Michigan and Eastern Michigan University, to illustrate their argument. Students at Eastern Michigan were receiving Pell grants at three times the amount the grants were distributed to students at Michigan. These same students were helping pay a $20 million subsidy to the athletics department, whereas their more affluent counterparts at Michigan paid nothing to support the much larger, more prestigious athletic department. More generally, the four conferences that have the highest rate of students on Pell grants (Conference USA, Western Athletic Conference, Sun Belt, and Mid-American) were all in the top five for athletic program subsidy rates.

Restated, the schools with the "poorest" students are relying on them to fund their hemorrhaging athletic departments, whereas wealthier students at

TABLE 2
Relation of Pell Grants to Athletic Subsidies

Conference	% Pell Grant Students	Total Expenses FTE ($)	Average Athletics Support per Student ($)
ACC	14.87	38,426	327
Big 12	16.42	27,622	130
Big 10	16.44	41,631	67
SEC	19.13	31,046	168
MWC	21.86	42,481	1,177
Pac-10	22.93	40,464	242
Big East	23.96	32,100	491
MAC	26.95	18,141	915
Sunbelt	30.41	14,553	559
WAC	30.47	24,472	718
C-USA	34.54	28,888	697

Source: Denhart & Vedder (2010).

institutions with overflowing resources are not forced to contribute to the athletic departments through fees or tuition allocation (see Table 2). What Denhart and Vedder (2010) failed to examine is the inequity in athletic subsidies that exists within the larger conferences. As stated earlier, only 13 athletic programs turned a profit in 2008, leaving a plethora of major college athletic departments that operate at a deficit or receive support from the parent university. Additionally, these schools are forced to compete with profit-making programs for recruits, in on-field competitions, and in the quality of facilities and institutional offerings they provide to the student-athletes. This competition between big-time college athletic programs has been popularly deemed the "arms race" and evidence suggests the race is accelerating rapidly with no end in sight.

Pushback Against University Support for Athletics

As outlined previously, universities are increasingly becoming entangled in a battle between academics and athletics, where the pressures to compete athletically are coinciding with legislatures that are reducing taxpayer funding of academic budgets at universities while raising tuition at record rates. Athletic expenditures have continued to rise as schools compete with one another for recruits, championships, and fans. However, athletic revenues are not increasing at a high enough pace to keep up with the expenses at most universities. This increasing gap between revenues and expenses is causing athletic departments to rely more heavily on financial support from the university through tuition reallocations and student fees. This reliance collides with cuts to public funding for universities and steady rises in tuition. Inevitably, university administrators and students have begun to push back against athletic departments receiving funding that could be used for academic purposes or to reduce the financial burden placed on university students.

Nationwide, donations, another major source of university revenue, have leveled off in the past 5 years. Total gifts to universities declined more than 11% from 2008 to 2009 and were the same amount in 2010 as they were in 2006 (Masterson, 2011). As university finances become further strained, it seems illogical for public money to be used to support unsustainable athletic departments. For example, Eichelberger and Young (2012) noted the amount of subsidy Rutgers University provided to its athletic department in 2010 would have been enough to hire 256 assistant professors or 132 full professors. Similarly, Branch (2011) noted the average compensation, when controlled for inflation, for head football coaches at public universities had grown by 750% since 1984, whereas the compensation for college professors has grown by a mere 32%.

Financial crises across U.S. universities are causing students to shoulder a greater financial load to support both the academic and athletic departments. Total student loan debt in the United States reached more than $1 trillion during 2012. Students are partially being targeted to cover these costs because they have little power to push back against the increases. Outside of not attending university, students have little power to stop increases in tuition, tuition reallocations, or student fees. They do not have veto power or, often, even a vote on matters dealing with how much they pay in tuition and how that money is ultimately spent. For example, students at Florida International University were not given any options to intervene against the $2 million the athletic department received of their tuition or opt out of the almost $17 million the athletic department collected in student fees in 2011.

Until now, legislators who have tried to give students more rights have been denied. In Kentucky, Representative Joni Jenkins filed a bill to prohibit public universities from charging commuter students athletics fees. Jenkins stated many residents from her district were part-time students who received absolutely no benefit from the athletics fee they were mandated to pay (Berkowitz et al., 2010). Although acknowledging that smaller schools rely on student fees to fund nonrevenue sports, she was pushing to give students in Kentucky the right to opt out of paying student fees. The state legislative committee never took up her bill.

In rare situations where students are given a voice, they have fought back against their tuition and fees being used to subsidize athletic departments. Student leaders at the University of Montana recently approved a $52 per year increase in athletics fees. However, the pushback against the annual increase in student fees was so great that the issue was put to a campus-wide vote and was eventually overturned by a two-to-one margin through the referendum. The student organization president stated the issue would be brought up again in the future because it was too risky to rely on ticket sales to fund the athletic department where sales have been shown to go down when teams are not successful (Berkowitz et al., 2010).

Parents who often help shoulder the financial burden of the tuition costs are also pushing back against athletics fees. Berkowitz and colleagues (2010) noted one student at Radford University was charged more than $5,000 in athletics fees during her time at the school. In a recent newspaper exposé on athletics fees the student's parents, who helped pay her tuition, chided: "[The student] does go to some of the games," parent Linda Randall stated, "but she's going there for the academics; she's not going to fund athletics" (quoted by Berkowitz et al., 2010, para. 8). Randall noted the fees would have been enough to afford off-campus rent or pay back loans and called the mandatory fee structure "disheartening."

University faculty members are also questioning the legitimacy of funding athletics with public money. In March 2012, the faculty council at Rutgers voted to "demand" cutting $5 million from the funding the university provides to athletics by 2016 along with an end to requiring students to pay athletics fees. The council supported the notion that college athletics had become what was described earlier as a "financial arms race" (Eichelberger & Young, 2012). The faculty eventually convinced the university to lower athletic subsidies by $1 million, but Rutgers made up for it by raising student fees by 3%. Students were not allowed to vote on the referendum to raise student fees. Similarly, Cincinnati faculty chairwoman Marla Hall stated, "we are concerned about the use of general fund money for anything that is not central to the academic mission of the university" (as quoted by Upton, Berkowitz, & Gillum, 2010, para. 7). Moreover, at the University of Texas at Austin, the faculty passed a resolution protesting the raise given to head football coach Mack Brown before the 2009 Bowl Championship Series (BCS) National Championship game.

Even with these pushbacks, it is obvious the popularity of athletics on college campuses among students, fans, and decision makers is trending upwards. Scholars and university administrators alike have defended the athletic departments' place within the university culture. Similarly, as evidenced next, even the harshest critics of college athletics have acknowledged the benefits of having a successful athletic department.

Positioning Big-Time Athletics

In his book *Branded Nation*, James Twitchell (2004) wrote athletic departments are often a university's "window to the world" (p. 116). In the book, Twitchell outlined how, during his time as a professor at the University of Florida, the athletic department quickly became *the* brand for the entire university. He stated most Floridians either love or hate the Gators, and the athletic department was an "easy identification" for fans. Moreover, he noted that outside of the university foundation building "where a statue of some illustrious donor or beloved professor would stand at an elite school, is a bronze statue of the athletic department's trademarked mascots, Albert and Alberta Alligator" (Twitchell, 2004, p. 115).

Similarly, in December 2011 Colorado State University President Tony Frank gave a speech addressing the role of athletics in the university setting. Frank (2011) stated the benefits athletics provides in terms of entertainment, alumni connections, and student life are commonly understood and accepted.

Additionally, he encouraged people to consider the role athletics play in the reputation of the university and attracting students to enroll in the school. Frank (2011) ended his speech by stating, "so, at the end of the day...I wind up thinking [Colorado State], including its reputation, needs successful athletic programs" (p. 3).

Even a group of Cal-Berkeley faculty members who were campaigning against university support of the athletic department acknowledged the role a well-managed athletics department can play in the university atmosphere. The group conceded athletics likely plays a significant role in academic fundraising numbers and "adds to campus spirit and unity, provides free advertising for the campus, helps in branding, and provides a link and outreach to alumni" (quoted in Berkowitz et al., 2010, para. 10). Similarly, Rutgers President Richard McCormick stated Rutgers athletics provided "positive branding, exposure and visibility for our university and the State of New Jersey" (quoted by Eichelberger & Young, 2012, p. 3).

Interestingly, credit agencies also believe athletic departments can improve the overall health of the university. Moody's Investor Services stated they consider the success of athletic programs when setting the credit score and interest rates universities receive. Weaver (2011) stated Moody's believed "a carefully managed, successful intercollegiate Division I athletics program can have a positive credit impact on a university" (p. 18). The author stated athletic departments often rely on these ratings to secure low-interest loans to finance various projects (e.g., stadium renovations) that are paid off over decades. The crossover between university and athletic department comes when the athletic department leverages university assets to secure lower interest rates for athletic projects (Weaver, 2011).

There is evidence to suggest that university administrators believe the prestige and benefits of having a successful athletic program increase if the university participates at the Division I level. Based on this premise, and even with small Division I schools struggling to make ends meet, Weaver (2011) noted there is still a long list of schools attempting to make the jump to the highest division. Weaver used the term "mission creep" to describe the desire of smaller schools to use athletics to enhance their status through association with larger schools. She stated Division I is being increasingly infiltrated by schools with less than 5,000 students like Lehigh and Saint Joseph's University. In fact, Presbyterian College, home of 1,200 students, transitioned to Division I in 2007–2008. That year, its men's basketball team was forced to play 25 road games to attract Division I opponents. Weaver (2011) believed Presbyterian was simply trying to keep pace with the schools located around them that had Division I status and prestige.

So many schools applied for Division I membership that the NCAA issued a 4-year moratorium on new membership that was in effect until August 2011. In a press release, the NCAA stated the moratorium was to review the requirements needed to be a Division 1 institution (Copeland, 2007). It was implied that new standards needed to be set to curb the mass migration of aspiring Division II schools to the Division I ranks.

> *Since 1986, 47 institutions have reclassified from Division II to Division I, including three institutions that completed the reclassification process and achieved active membership this year. Another 18 former Division II institutions currently are at various stages of the reclassification process—including six that officially are entering exploratory membership this year. Five institutions are entering Year 1 of provisional membership, two are entering Year 2, three are entering Year 3 and two are entering Year 4—the final phase before gaining active membership. Two institutions currently are joining Division I from outside the NCAA. One is beginning exploratory membership this year; the other is in the fifth year of a six-year provisional membership. (Copeland, 2007, para. 13–14)*

Some universities have even chosen to openly invest heavily in the athletic department in hopes of raising the school's national profile. The administration at Western Kentucky University provided the athletic department with $14 million of the $19 million they needed to operate in 2010, money that came directly from the general operating budget of the university. This followed the football team joining Division I in 2009. University spokesperson Bob Skipper believed the athletics program brought much needed attention to the entire university.

> *WKU's appearance in the 2012 NCAA men's basketball tourna-*
> *ment and WKU's football success last season has brought national*
> *exposure to the university that cannot be purchased. The exposure*
> *has resulted in increased interest by prospective students, instilled a*
> *renewed sense of pride in the university, and has elevated general*
> *awareness of WKU at the state and national level. (as quoted by*
> *Blackford, 2012, p. 2)*

Professor Murray Sperber, an outspoken critic of the overcommercialization of college athletics, called the belief that athletic success leads to university recognition "The Flutie Factor." Sperber stated applications to Boston College University went up by 25% after quarterback Doug Flutie completed a Hail Mary pass to beat the University of Miami in 1984. The game was nationally televised on Thanksgiving Day, and Boston College was a massive underdog to the Hurricanes. It has been posited that the game put the small Catholic college "on the map" and that the school enjoyed increased application numbers in the years after the game (Sperber, 2000).

Sperber (2000) further observed university administrators turned "The Flutie Factor" concept into "mission-driven" athletics. He stated this mission meant schools promoted their big-time sports programs no matter the cost because athletics were an essential part of the university mission. In fact, Sperber (2000) found that prospective students were often equating athletic success to academic prestige of the university. Students with higher standardized test scores that apply to weaker academic schools because of the athletic department were coined the "Flutie Cohort." Further, he found 88% of males and 51% of females were "well informed" of the football and/or men's basketball team when they decided to enroll in a Division I university. Conversely, males and females both answered negatively more than 50% of the time to the question, "When applying to colleges for admission, how well informed were you about the undergraduate education programs of the schools to which you applied?" (Sperber, 2000, p. 62).

As Branch (2011) described, college athletics are "deeply inscribed in the culture of our nation. Half a million [people] play competitive intercollegiate sports ... millions of spectators flock into football stadiums each Saturday in the fall, and tens of millions more watch on television" (p. 3). Most university administrators fundamentally believe a successful athletic department is a monstrous competitive advantage and gives universities a sense of legitimacy, positive press, and exposure to a group of prospective students and boosters who may never know about their university without the athletic department. However, the future of nonrevenue sports is not as clear.

As evidenced by the Cal-Berkeley example, eliminating nonrevenue sports is often the first step athletic programs take when they are forced to cut their budget. The message sent by Cal-Berkeley administrators who threw their clout behind building a new football stadium while ignoring the fundraising efforts of those trying to save the five eliminated sports should not be ignored. The athletic funding crunch will have a great impact on the athletes, coaches, and administrators of nonrevenue sports. Some may argue that this is but a harsh reality of the contemporary higher education; nonrevenue sports should be eliminated if the department is struggling to meet their budget. However, as noted earlier, a finite amount of athletic teams actually generate enough revenue to subsidize themselves. In essence, all but 30 or so athletic teams (an approximate estimation of the amount of men's basketball and football teams that generate more revenue than they spend) cost their athletic department money.

The athletic funding crisis is a real and continuing problem. Against this backdrop of the university's—and athletics program's—budgetary shortcomings, whereby universities and athletic department have hit an impasse in which both parties are under increased scrutiny to justify their financial independence from taxpayer dollars, the role of boosters has become increasingly critical. The use of public funds and student fees to fund athletic departments is being routinely criticized and limited by state legislators. If legislative and public higher education budgets continue to tighten, it is not hard to imagine tuition reallocations and student athletic fees becoming obsolete as funding options for college athletics. One way in which universities have attempted to combat this gap is through the "corporatization" of higher education and intercollegiate athletics.

Many scholars have examined the corporatization of higher education and college athletics. For example, Murray Sperber published *College Sports Inc.* in

1990 and *Beer and Circus* in 2000, Henry Giroux published *The University in Chains: Confronting the Military-Industrial-Academic Complex* in 2007, and James Twitchell published *Branded Nation* in 2004. This corporatization has come in many forms, from turning campuses into veritable shopping malls to changing the operating structures of educational institutions to align more with private sector corporations. In *The University in Chains*, Henry Giroux stated anyone who spends time on a college campus cannot help but notice how the culture and polity of higher education is changing. Specifically, Giroux (2007) believed universities are becoming increasingly corporatized. Professors are now expected to be "academic entrepreneurs" where the money and prestige they bring the university is more important than their ability to educate the students (Giroux, 2007). Further, Ohmann (2002, as cited by Giroux, 2007) posited corporate universities operate like profit-generating organizations that are becoming less concerned with their contribution to the betterment of society and more concerned with their profit generating ability.

Giroux (2007) believed this was evidenced by universities increasingly adopting the logics and practices of corporations in their everyday activities and selling off anything they could to private corporations in order to improve their bottom line. Private corporations that pay the university for access to their students are increasingly running bookstores, housing services, and dining halls on college campuses. He compared the atmosphere of selling on a college campus to a local shopping mall: "Universities and colleges compound this marriage of commercial and educational values by signing exclusive contracts with Pepsi, Nike, and other contractors, further blurring the distinction between student and consumer" (Giroux, 2007, pp. 105–106). In this vein, Twitchell (2004) stated that during his tenure the University of Florida student union had come to resemble a department store, and Bok (2003, p. 3) listed the ways this commercialization has been manifested in the higher education setting:

1. The influence of economic forces on universities (e.g., the growth of computer science majors and departments)

2. The influence of the surrounding corporate culture (e.g., the increased use on campuses of terms such as chief executive officer, bottom line, or brand name)
3. The influence of student career interests on the curriculum (e.g., more vocational courses)
4. Efforts to economize the in-university expenditures (hiring more adjunct teachers) or to use administrative methods adapted from business
5. Attempts to quantify matters within the university that are not truly quantifiable, such as trying to express matters of value in monetary terms rather than qualitatively

David Kirp (2003) referred to this shift in priorities on college campuses as "The New U" (p. 1). In *Shakespeare, Einstein, and the Bottom Line: The Marketing of Higher Education*, Kirp (2003) argued higher education is being "transformed by both the power and the ethic of the marketplace" (p. 2). He surmised famed institutions like the University of Chicago were beginning to look more and more like Hamburger University, McDonald's corporate training program:

> *To speak of McDonald's and the University of Chicago in the same breath is blasphemy, at least in Hyde Park. But the rise to prominence of schools like Hamburger U—not your father's higher education, certainly, but an accredited institution nonetheless—as well as the hard choices that confront a quintessential academy of higher learning like Chicago illustrate a much larger phenomenon. (Kirp, 2003, p. 1)*

Further, Kirp (2003) believed that the role of the university president had been altered in the corporate university model. Previously, presidents were expected to exhibit strong leadership skills while overseeing the daily operations of university. Now, they had less presence within the institution because they are "consumed with the never-ending task of raising money" (Kirp, 2003, p. 4). Similarly, Bok (2003) posited:

> *The obvious culprits (to blame for the commercialization of higher education) were university presidents and their*

entourage of bureaucratic helpers. Intent upon accumulating money to expand the size and reputation of the institution, campus administrators were forever forcing the methods of the marketplace on a reluctant community of scholars. (p. 4)

The revenue-generating model of higher education also transformed the classes students were required to take to obtain a degree. Instead of "molding students into citizens of the republic" (Kirp, 2003, p. 258), universities are increasingly allowing students to specialize and only take the courses they want or (believe they) need. Kirp (2003) surmised:

In most schools ... the common core has been abandoned in favor of innocuous "distribution requirements" that turn higher education into a shopping mall. Much like Swiss watchmakers, today's liberal arts professors offer what is widely regarded as a luxury item to a shrinking clientele ... Career-minded graduates have shifted their allegiance to the "practical arts." (pp. 258–259)

Many scholars and commentators have similarly argued that much like the broader university structure, athletic departments are also becoming increasingly corporatized. Bok (2003) called college athletics "the oldest form of commercialization in American higher education" (p. 35), and Tsitsos and Nixon (2012) stated the "commercial athletic marketplace has evolved into the 21st century. We now refer to 'big time' intercollegiate athletics involving investments of many millions of dollars in the operations, staffing, facilities, and student athletes in college sports" (p. 69). Similarly, Smith (2012) argued administrative titles in athletic departments now mirror those seen in the business world with schools often having a chief financial officer and an extensive fundraising staff.

In his essay "The Shame of College Athletics," Taylor Branch (2011) stated "corporations offer money so they can profit from the glory of college athletes, and the universities grab it" (p. 2). Athletic departments have replaced iconic, intimate facilities with spacious, corporatized arenas in the name of revenue generation (see Louisville's construction of the KFC Yum!

Center to replace Freedom Hall, an arena the men's basketball teams had competed in for 54 years while ranking in the top five for attendance for the last 29 years). Similarly, athletic departments are increasingly entering into exclusive apparel licensing agreements with clothing, equipment, and footwear companies and selling their marketing rights to megacorporations like IMG. Further, the University of Texas signed an agreement with ESPN to start its own television network, "The Longhorn Network." Under the terms of the deal, the University of Texas will be paid $11 million annually for 20 years. Marketing executive Sonny Vaccaro, who signed Michael Jordan to his first footwear endorsement deal, spoke to the money grab he believed universities were engaged in when he testified in front of the Knight Commission on Intercollegiate Athletics.

> *"I'm not hiding," Vaccaro told a closed hearing at the Willard Hotel in Washington, D.C., in 2001. "We want to put our materials on the bodies of your athletes, and the best way to do that is buy your school. Or buy your coach."... "Why," asked Bryce Jordan, the president emeritus of Penn State, "should a university be an advertising medium for your industry?" Vaccaro did not blink. "They shouldn't sir," he replied. "You sold your souls, and you're going to continue selling them. You can be very moral and righteous in asking me that question, sir," Vaccaro added with irrepressible good cheer, "but there's not one of you in this room that's going to turn down any of our money. You're going to take it. I can only offer it." (Branch, 2011, p. 2)*

Further, Branch (2011) emphasized how corporations profit from unpaid college athletes by stating anyone who surveys the college athletics scene will "catch an unmistakable whiff of the plantation" (p. 5). Although Branch (2011) was specifically referring to the exploitation of unpaid college athletes, the analogy can be extended to include corporate profitization from reallocations of tuition and collection of fees from the student body. By following the chain of money, it is evident the aforementioned student fees and tuition reallocations collected from university students are ultimately leading to profits for private corporations through, among other things, postseason tournaments and bowl games, sponsorship agreements, broadcast rights, and commercial advertising.

In 2011–2012, the student athletic fees at the University of Cincinnati supported programs that were ultimately used by Adidas to promote and sell its shoes and apparel, corporate bowl games sponsors to sell advertising and television rights, and the Big East Conference to sell sponsorship packages. The Big East Conference has numerous corporate sponsors, including American Eagle, Geico, and Reese's. The Cincinnati football team played in the AutoZone Liberty Bowl, a game broadcast on ESPN that was sponsored by corporations such as AutoZone, FedEx, and Quaker State. Similarly, Giroux and Searls Giroux (2012) stated high-profile athletic departments "engage in a number of interlocking campus relationships with private sector corporations" (p. 269).

> *Lucrative deals that generate massive revenue are made through media contracts involving television broadcasts, video games, and Internet programming. Substantial profits flow in from merchandizing football goods, signing advertising contracts, and selling an endless number of commodities from toys to alcoholic beverages and fast food at the stadium, tailgating parties and sports bars. (p. 269)*

Conclusion

Detailed examples of the reclassification of the University of New Orleans from Division I to Division III, the program cuts at the University of California-Berkeley, the reliance of Virginia colleges and universities on student fees for athletic department funding, and the national exposure of Western Kentucky University based on recent athletic success all showcase the various ways funding can dramatically alter the outlook of any athletic department. These examples also illustrate the importance of athletic department officials to be in tune with the current condition of their own athletic department in order to be best prepared for the future. We argue that this general awareness of the pulse of intercollegiate athletics is not new. Since the formalization of the NCAA in the early 1900s, actions by government officials (e.g., President Theodore Roosevelt), university administrators (e.g., the Chancellor of New York University), and athletic directors (e.g., former Rutgers athletic director Tim Pernetti) indicate there has been little debate about the *awareness* of the pulse of college athletics. However, there notably have been overt decisions to ultimately prioritize commercialization and revenue generation.

Each of the seven public universities that spent more than $100 million in athletic expenses during the 2011–2012 academic year (*USA Today*, 2012) relied on an average of $31 million in athletic department contributions (i.e., booster donations) to offset some of these costs. Additionally, these athletic departments remain more purely self-sustaining because they received less than a 5% subsidy in "allocated" funds from the university. Paramount to this discussion of strategies athletic departments use to combat rising costs in college athletics is the reliance on these allocated funds. Intentionally an all-encompassing term, allocated sources include any form of money given to the athletic department from student fees, a direct transfer from the university, and any other subsidy from the university of state government to augment athletic department revenue. Schools such as Coppin State, Mississippi Valley State, North Carolina Asheville, and Maryland-Eastern Shore all relied on allocated funds to account for more than half of their athletic department revenue (Bass & Newman, 2013). Although it is important to note the gaping disparity from a pure numbers standpoint in revenue and expenses based on the athletic prominence of the school (e.g., the University of Texas having more than $100 million in expenses and Coppin State having less than $5 million), the percentage of booster donations that each of these schools receives provides even more powerful evidence of the drastic economic disparity that does exist across the spectrum of Division I athletics.

This trend to increasingly rely on allocated funding to prop up athletic department revenue serves as arguably the purest example of the entangled relationship between athletic departments and university administrators. Specifically, Drape (2010) aptly pointed out that FBS athletic departments spent 10% more in 2009 than they did in 2008. During that same time span, those same FBS athletic departments received 28% more in allocated funds from the university. These statistics certainly add credence to university naysayers who lament giving more money to athletics while simultaneously cutting academic programs. Additionally, in a time when athletic departments are experiencing a funding crisis, the universities are transferring more of the financial burden to the students themselves to combat the funding crises the actual universities are experiencing. Thus, many students are victims of the financial funding fallout from two different angles: increased student fees to help subsidize the athletic department and increased tuition to lessen the financial load borne by the university. A closer look at this corporatization in the university setting at large is merited.

The Role of Athletics in the Corporatized University

I N THE PRECEDING TWO CHAPTERS, we provided an understanding for how college athletics developed and how it fits within larger machinations of higher education funding today. Particularly, the first chapter provided a historic overview of the NCAA in order to explicate three changes that occurred in the 1970s and 1980s, "systemic, groundbreaking, and relatively simultaneous key movements [that] helped to dramatically change the dynamic of the NCAA" (p. 8). First, we examined the split of the NCAA into three major divisions in the early 1970s. This fundamentally arranged the universities into Division I, II, and III. The divisions functioned in such a way that Division I schools provide scholarships to athletes, Division II provides partial scholarships, and Division III does not provide any scholarships for participating in athletics (Yost, 2010).

Next, we laid out how Title IX affected college athletics and how it continues to affect it today. The requirement for all universities and athletics departments to make opportunities equal for both men and women greatly altered the funding landscape for athletics. Third, the first chapter examined the importance of media contracts. Since the mid-1980s, media contracts have played a large role in funding of college athletics and competition, particularly among conferences. All of these events changed the landscape of college athletics, making it even more of a commercial entity. In this way, the shift in the 1970s and 1980s was similar to the alteration in the framework of higher education in society more generally. That is to say, all of these systemic changes came at a time when women were becoming more active in the workforce, for example, and higher education was turning toward the corporate university model. In the second chapter, we focused on how these changes have affected college athletics. The corporatization of funding, wherein more of the burden for financing is put on the individual tuition payer and private funding sources, has had a great impact on college athletics. In the second chapter, we showed how this can affect universities, such as the University of New Orleans. When enrollment decreased because of Hurricane Katrina, the university and the athletics department suffered. They were unable to make up in fees what they were spending due to the lack of attendance, and private sources of funding were tied into fixing the local community. Despite the university administrators knowing that the athletics department should drop from Division I to Division III due to an annual deficit in excess of $1 million, and the initial decision to drop to Division III, the University of New Orleans ultimately decided to stay in Division I by raising student fees for athletics.

The first two chapters focus on how systemic changes in society, from positive social changes in equal rights to improving technology and media saturation to new ideologies in public funding, have altered college athletics. The historic narrative and examples in the first two chapters can all be attributed to systemic changes over time. In this third chapter, we focus on how we can understand this system from a theoretically informed viewpoint. Specifically, we call upon classical political economists to enlighten the discourse around the continued need for each university to keep up in the arms race—colloquially referred to as "keeping up with the Joneses." The chapter begins by first tying political economic theory to what we examined in the second chapter in particular.

Increased Corporatization in Higher Education

As illustrated in the second chapter, the schema of higher education has witnessed a gradual shift in recent decades from a focus on learning defended by academicians and governmental support to a corporate approach focused on building relationships with corporate entities (Williams, 2001). Slaughter and Rhoades (2000) explained that the restructuring of higher education has mirrored government: "With government, agencies and activities addressing the general welfare have been downsized, while those concerned with corporate competitiveness or corporate welfare have been expanded" (p. 73). Taking a critical lens, Giroux (2010) proclaimed that this shift in higher education toward a corporate university "places an emphasis on winning at all costs, a ruthless competitiveness, hedonism, the cult of individualism, and a subject largely constructed within a market-driven rationality that abstracts economics and markets from ethical considerations" (p. 185).

The shift from reliance on government aid to a focus on corporate and private relationships not only fits within the corporate university framework but also reflects the culture of major intercollegiate athletics in the university system. In 2011, university athletics departments increased revenue generated by $190 million spending an additional $267 million when compared with 2010 (Upton & Berkowitz, 2012). In 2012, 13 teams generated more than $100 million of revenue per year with departments attempting to become more privatized in their revenue generation, up from 10 teams in 2011 (Berkowitz et al., 2014).

As elucidated in the previous chapter, for the schools with the largest budgets seeking to keep up with the other largest athletics departments, the revenue is being increased through monies garnered from outside (e.g., noninstitutional, nongovernmental) sources. For example, schools that have been successful on a national stage in a sport such as football, which brings in the most revenue in the majority of athletics departments, have been able to support themselves with a continually declining percentage of subsidies. Data obtained by *USA Today* (Berkowitz et al., 2014) from the 225 universities with an obligation to report revenue data indicate that the highest percentage of subsidies provided for an athletics department taking in more than $70 million a year (37 teams) was the University of Virginia at 16.24% of total revenue provided by university subsidy. Further, Ohio State University, the University of Oklahoma, Pennsylvania State University, Louisiana State University, and the University of Texas all generated more than $100 million in 2012 while taking zero subsidies. Walker (1994) suggested that this increase in tax-cutting legislation and reliance on outside sources has placed an enlarged pressure on athletic development offices as entities that now work outside of the institutions' development offices.

Yet, as there seems to be a large trend for schools to seek outside funds from boosters, as noted in the second chapter, smaller schools are simultaneously increasing student fees. Although it appears here that these "subsidies" are governmental in nature because they come from the school, this does not go against the national trend that suggests capital can be gained for the most powerful via subsidies from the poorest (Loveridge & Nizalov, 2007). The clamoring for funding has met a perfect storm of governmental structure that privileges private capital accumulation (Cummings, 1988) on the back of public policy designed to accentuate economic development above all else (Harvey, 2006).

This is not an entirely new phenomenon and in fact traces back to the early 20th century when economic divergence was highest in the developed world based on government structure prioritizing private capital accumulation, a trend that has reemerged since 1980 (Piketty, 2014). Benford (2007) noted that as far back as the 1920s, individuals were clamoring over and discussing the commercial focus of college athletics. Citing Savage (1929, p. ix), Benford reiterated, "[College football] is not a student's game as it once was. It is a highly organized commercial enterprise . . . The great matches are highly profitable" (p. 6). Further, Zimbalist (1999) elucidated that commercialism and profit have been one of the driving sources behind corruption in college athletics. The opportunity for commercial success and revenue has continued with the advent of new media contracts over the course of the past three decades since the decision of the Supreme Court in *NCAA vs. The Board of Regents of University of Oklahoma* (1984) wherein the NCAA member institutions were given the rights to negotiate television contracts. The ability for institutions and member conferences by proxy to negotiate media contracts has been financially advantageous for the five major conferences (Southeastern Conference, Big 10, Big 12, Pac-12, and Atlantic Coast Conference) which have increased revenues greatly based largely upon television contracts such as the Pac-12's latest agreement totaling $4.3 billion—paying each university roughly $30 million per year (Dent, 2012). Assuredly, this frenzy for money aligns well with the ideals of college athletics. As Roger

Pielke (2011) pointed out in his *The New York Times* blog, "The Supreme Court has called the N.C.A.A. 'an association of schools which compete against each other to attract television revenues, not to mention fans and athletes.'"

In the current landscape of college athletics, every wall, timeout, scoreboard, and jersey comes complete with its own advertising opportunity, which further perpetuates this corporatization of college athletics. Other schools see the prosperous large schools and want to try to keep up with the Joneses—what Veblen (1899/2007) refers to as the leisure class. Benford (2007) explained:

> *Sports reform activists point out that nowhere is the increasing commercialization of college sports more evident than in the "college athletics arms race." If Nebraska builds new sky boxes or adds a new weight room, Oklahoma, Colorado, and Texas will no doubt follow suit. One sports reformer I interviewed refers to this as an 'edifice complex.' The ensuing competition leaves most programs, even many of the richest ones, swimming in a sea of red ink and in search of new sources of revenue. (p. 10)*

Scholars such as Giroux (2010), Slaughter and Rhoades (2000), Williams (2001), Benford (2007), and Zimbalist (1999) provide valuable insight into the corporate university landscape and the role of funding within this institutional framework. Yet, even as the discourse surrounding athlete "entitlements" and corporate institutions continues and indeed has grown following the approved unionization of Northwestern University student-athletes (explained in greater detail in the fourth chapter), there have been few attempts at synthesizing literature and developing an understanding for the impact of the "arms race" on the solvency of college athletics as it rests within the corporate university. And, at the same time, there is little acknowledgement for how this "arms race" fits within the general framework of free-market competition. Therefore, this chapter is an endeavor to examine the political economics of big-time college athletics in an attempt to offer a theoretical explanation neither condemning nor accepting the current status of intercollegiate athletics. Our task in this chapter is to understand how the general framework of intercollegiate athletics makes sense when considered within the historical present (e.g., the corporate university) and what this ultimately means for the parties involved.

Understanding college athletics within this framework laid out in the second chapter, we use political economic theory to build upon the necessary elements of corporate university, marketization, competition, and winning at all costs as these ideologies relate to Veblen's (1901/2007) leisure class while leaning on classical political economists' (e.g., Smith, Ricardo, and Polanyi) ideas of the shame of relative poverty related to the college "arms race" and labor market theory. In building upon our earlier discussion in the second chapter on how the market rationality has come to dominate the landscape of college athletics as it sits within the corporate university, we seek to move toward an understanding for how these rationalities affect competition between institutions and the athlete as laborer. In so doing, we provide examples of the arms race in college athletics to show how this market rationality has taken hold while examining who benefits from this corporate landscape and so-called "arms race." In order to accomplish this, we consider the contracts and pay structures in college athletics as we question who the benefactors are within this schema.

In order to address both the institutional competition and the athlete labor market as a part of this competition, we will use Texas A&M as a case study. First, we provide a layout of the political economy of "keeping up" as it relates to both institutional competition and the athlete labor market. Next, we explicitly interrogate the political economics of "keeping up" in college athletics by examining institutional competition commonly known as the "arms race." Then, we consider athletes as commodity by reviewing the political economy of the labor market and extending the ideology of "keeping up" to explain the student athlete in this schema by examining a case study of Texas A&M and former student-athlete, Johnny Manziel. We conclude by offering some implications for the future of college athletics as they continue upon this course toward unfettered free-market ideologies that assesses qualities of worthiness to some and disposability to others.

The Political Economy of "Keeping Up"

To understand the "keeping up" that defines intercollegiate athletics in the current moment, we begin by considering Veblen's (1901/2007) theory of the leisure class. For Veblen, the leisure class itself is composed of the historic class of nobles, priests, and their accompanying people—what today, and when he was writing in 1901, can be thought of as elite business leaders and other members of the upper class. Present in all iterations of humanity throughout history, "the institution of a leisure class is the outgrowth of an early discrimination between employments, according to which some employments are worth and others unworthy" (Veblen, 1901/2007, p. 11). He explained that people or classes in society can be understood as different from one another by their activity—some being the animate and others, inert. The concept of animate includes "such things as in the apprehension of the animistic savage or barbarian are formidable by virtue of a real or imputed habit of initiating action" (Veblen, 1901/2007, p. 13). Thus, the animate belongs to the active, moving entity that directs teleological activities—directed toward an end. For something to be inert is the complete opposite; there is not a final cause and there is nothing actually being done. This distinction is what Veblen perceives drives the division of labor throughout history. That is, some employment practices are thought to move society toward a particular end—the animate—whereas other jobs are viewed as inert, or lacking valuable purpose. These concepts in history are socially constructed and hold great power in deciding what and who is valued in a society. As society progressed from original hunter-gatherer colonies, the difference between animate and inert groups was divided into two classes, industry and exploit.

Industry "is effort that goes to create a new thing, with a new purpose given to it by the fashioning of hand of its maker out of passive ('brute') material; while exploit, so far as it results in an outcome useful to the agent, is the conversion to his own ends of energies previously directed to some other end by another agent" (Veblen, 1901/2007, p. 14). The exploited one is typically "stouter, more massive, better capable of sudden and violent strain, and more readily inclined to self-assertion, active emulation, and aggression" (Veblen, 1901/2007, p. 14). This original distinction between those with the ability to function differently continues to widen as "a cumulative process of selective adaptation to the new distribution of employments will set in" (Veblen, 1901/2007, p. 14). What occurs, then, is a widening division in societies based upon what attributes are privileged in a given society. For example, in a hunter-gatherer society, the strong men are privileged, and continue to be privileged, as they are unwilling to give up their rank, and develop the future generation to be good at the same things that are privileged. Once entrenched deeply within a society, the able-bodied must destroy competitors and elude those who try to reduce their significance. For those on the outside looking in, *they seek to emulate those that do have power.* This is the crux of the leisure class that Veblen builds upon.

Having an understanding for the more primitive societies, it is important to note how these conditions of emulation change as societies themselves change. As emulation continues to occur and the stronger continue to defeat the weak, aggression becomes the key element of success and those qualities and life goods acquired by seizure are as valid as those earned. Thus, it becomes a society based upon the idea that "obtaining goods by other methods than seizure comes to be accounted unworthy of man in his best estate" (Veblen, 1901/2007, p. 17). This means, then, that exploitation by seizing upon the work of another agent is more noble than industrial employment and those noted as honorable simply have superior force to those industrial men who are conversely dishonorable. So, we consider that the capitalist who invests money into workers and gaining a surplus value through their labor is seizing upon the work of another agent and is viewed more highly in society. Simply, the wealthy man is viewed as more desirable than the working class man. Put differently, "Arms are honorable, and the use of them, even in seeking the life of the meanest creatures of the fields becomes a honorific employment. At the same time, employment in industry becomes correspondingly odious, and, in the common-sense apprehension, the handling of the tools and implements of industry falls beneath the dignity of able-bodied men. Labor becomes irksome" (Veblen, 1901/2007, p. 18). Although Veblen discusses at length the idea of combat and conquest, what he is really trying to drive home is an overall frame of mind that becomes a predatory attitude. Veblen (1901/2007) stated, "Predation cannot become the habitual, conventional resource of any group or any class until industrial methods have been developed to such a degree of efficiency as to leave a margin worth fighting for, above the subsistence of those engaged in getting a living" (p. 19).

Starting from this understanding, we can begin to negotiate how the leisure class sits within society today. The idea from Veblen (1901/2007) is that the predatory culture works best once there has been a growth in technology and efficiency. Here, we can relate Veblen to what Marx (1976) was talking about when he suggested that technology and efficiency actually work to further divide society. In today's world, technology divides and those who arise on top seek to keep control—similar to a barbaric society. By staying on top, the agent as a capitalist has the opportunity to exploit the industrial agent. Thus, those who sit within the leisure society are literally not contributing to the physical production of material and are not, by Veblen's definition, doing anything active or animate. Instead, they are being inert. Through this inert existence, the leisurely have the opportunity to increase their freedoms while diminishing the freedoms of others.

Living above "subsistence" and creating capital from the labors of others create the leisure society. The leisure society relates to the concept of relative deprivation insofar as, "social comparisons between people (as individuals or groups) are at the heart of relative deprivation" (Walker & Smith, 2002, p. 4). In contemporary America, scholars have found through studying relative deprivation, "that people's reactions to objective circumstances depend on their subjective comparisons" (Walker & Smith, 2002, p. 1). Relative deprivation has been contested in terms of applicability to different types of circumstances, but Crosby (1982) determined that only two conditions need to be met in order for one to feel a sense of relative deprivation: "wanting what one does not have, and feeling that one deserves whatever it is one wants but does not have" (Walker & Smith, 2002, p. 2). Relative deprivation also requires that individuals or groups compare themselves with others (Tougas & Beaton, 2002). Although political economists such as Sen (1983) argue against policy decisions based on the idea of relative deprivation in favor of absolute deprivation in order to focus on building capabilities, Sen argues "that absolute deprivation in terms of a person's capabilities relates to relative deprivation in terms of commodities, incomes and resources" (p. 153). Thus, the focus of relative deprivation is not necessarily refined only to subsistence, but to perceptions of justice and equality.

Importantly, the theory of relative deprivation has to do in large part with an individual's perceptions, not necessarily an objective experience. Sen (1983) is quick to point out that both absolute and relative poverty can lead to shame. Using Adam Smith's argument on the concept of necessities in *The Wealth of Nations*, Sen uses Smith's example of the leather shoe as a necessity in late 19th century England to state:

> *In this view to be able to avoid shame, an eighteenth century Englishman has to have leather shoes. It may be true that this situation has come to pass precisely because the typical members of that community happen to possess leather shoes, but the person in question needs leather shoes not so much to be less ashamed than others—that relative question is not even posed by Adam Smith—but simply not to be ashamed, which as an achievement is an absolute one.* (p. 160)

As societies progress, the necessities to avoid shame increase—much like in college football, the necessities to compete constantly increase. This is a commodity requirement relative to others in a given time and space (Sen, 1983), not something necessary to avoid absolute poverty, inherently. The commodity form is about avoiding shame. Because all are about perceptions and truths relative to others in society and affect how people live, shame, relative deprivation, and the idea of attempting to keep up with the leisure class all tie together and have very real consequences for the choices that people make.

To be clear, we are not suggesting that relative deprivation or shame in the classical sense of important issues such as world health and poverty are on par with perceptions of relative deprivation leading to athletics departments keeping up with one another or athletes pay schemes. Decidedly, we are not interested in absolute poverty, either—our goal is not to consider sport in the same vein as absolute poverty resulting in loss of abilities to function in the world. Rather, here, we are suggesting that these classical ideologies and prognostication of human behavior in a particular set of political economic conditions and structures can be helpful in explaining the overall movements and decisions of athletics departments and why or how it is possible that athletics departments make money off an athlete who does not receive compensation above or beyond his or her scholarship. Indeed, it is not our intention to argue for or against large capital investments by athletics departments or paying of players. Rather, these theoretical underpinnings are used to make sense of the current landscape of college athletics in totality.

Extending this to athletics in the corporate university, advertisers, businessmen, athletics directors, coaches, and university administrators work to attract athletes and differentiate themselves by capital campaigns to finance new buildings, facilitate championships, attract boosters and athletes, and so on. Therefore, to avoid shame, keep up with the elite (leisure class), and remain on a relative playing field, one who sees that new weight room or stadium the successful athletics department built must play its game and make money for itself. This is done precisely because a contradiction exists in the quest for all teams to have the best and newest facilities, there is a natural flow of the capitalist system, someone is always winning, whereas others are losing or at the very least, not winning as much (Harvey, 2006). Thus, the individual, the corporation, or, in our case, the athletics departments must always attempt to keep up with the most accomplished if they intend to win, but it is mathematically impossible for all to succeed.

There is no shortage of examples that can be utilized for evaluating the current status of college athletics as a site for keeping up with the leisure class. Those at the bottom will always try to emulate those at the top (Veblen, 1901/2007). In college athletics, this requires that athletics departments keep up with the best equipment, the best conferences with the biggest media contracts, and best facilities. The myriad reasons for involvement from television networks and apparel companies seem clear—there is a lot of money to be made. In fact, there are so many opportunities to be had that universities outsource their decision making to various sport management and marketing groups. Like the outsourcing of research and contract labor Giroux (2009) spoke about, these agreements are results driven and those results are defined by profit. In order to keep a simplified and cohesive nature to this chapter and the larger argument, we present the example of Texas A&M in their change to the Southeastern Conference (SEC) and building of new weight room and stadium, first. We then turn to the role of athletes in this schema, laying a foundation on a few examples of the industry surrounding college athletes, then primarily explicating the star quarterback during Texas A&M's move to the SEC, Johnny Manziel, and the attendant controversies surrounding his career.

"Keeping Up" in College Athletics

To understand Texas A&M's move to the SEC, it is important to first acknowledge the context in which this move took place. After all, as noted previously, keeping up in society whether analyzed through the scope of the leisure class (elites) or relative deprivation requires that one knows the context that precipitates an individual's or group's feeling of inequality or what fuels the competition. In this case, the moves toward conference realignment really began to enter into the discussion with the formation of the Big Ten Network that launched in 2007. The Big Ten Network was launched in a joint venture between Fox and the Big Ten in order to "provide the conference with more national exposure for Big Ten sports while enhancing its existing television agreements with its other television partners" (BTN: Big Ten Network, 2014). This new deal allowed the Big Ten schools to receive the largest television payouts of any conference-affiliated schools (Taylor, 2012).

The launch of a Big Ten Network and the coupled increase of television revenue seemed to begin an era of new television contracts larger than had ever before been seen. With the advent of the Big Ten Network, others soon sought to join them. The Pac-12 and SEC both have their own networks. (The Big 12 made a different agreement that will be brought to the forefront shortly.) These new contracts allowed the five major conferences (Southeastern Conference, Big 10, Big 12, Pac-12, and Atlantic Coast Conference) to distance themselves based in part on the revenue and exposure from television contracts such as the Pac-12's agreement totaling $4.3 billion—paying each university roughly $30 million per year (Dent, 2012).

At the same time, this arms race for television revenues took place in the context of posturing for university athletics departments to participate in Bowl Championship Series (BCS) bowls, which carried a much larger dividend for participation and exposure than the average bowl game. The issue went all the way to a hearing on Capitol Hill. Utah Senator Orrin Hatch responded to Utah's exclusion from a BCS game by proclaiming, "Frankly, there's an arrogance about the BCS that just drives me nuts. ... Hopefully this hearing will open the door to have some people reconsider their positions. And if nothing else, the Justice Department ought to be looking at this" (Frommer, 2009, para. 3). Even President Obama chimed in by suggesting that there should be a playoff providing all teams with an even chance for inclusion, which has now come to fruition.

The concern about being left out came to a head in 2010 when it became clear to conference commissioners and members that it was important to expand conference footprints into large media markets and position the schools and conferences for the best possible media contracts and opportunities to have the most exposure, be it through nationally televised games, more prestigious bowl opportunities, or the long-term sustainability that both of these avenues offer. Pertinent to our conversation here, which primarily focuses on Texas A&M, Nebraska was the first of the major dominoes to fall in June 2010 with the announcement that Nebraska would leave the Big 12 for the Big 10, citing the sustainability of the Big 10 (Kerkhoff, 2010). At the same time, Colorado left for the Pac-10 (now 12) with rumors that Texas, Texas Tech, Oklahoma, and Oklahoma State would soon follow (Carlton, 2010). However, just days later, that deal fell through when Texas, with the help of "business executives, conference commissioners, athletic directors, network executives with ties throughout college athletics, administrators at many levels throughout the NCAA membership" (Katz, 2010, para. 3), decided to stay with the Big 12. Oklahoma, Texas Tech, and Oklahoma State all decided to back out of the deal as well due in part to a plan for a new media contract that would net teams between $20 million and $25 million a year (Katz, 2010).

It is suspected that Texas stayed in part because of an agreement with ESPN to launch a separate "Longhorn Network" on an exclusive deal providing $300 million over 20 years to Texas, instead of starting a Big 12 network. This move caused Oklahoma and Texas A&M to consider a move to the SEC (Ubben, 2011), with Texas A&M ultimately deciding to move and Missouri following them shortly after. According to Texas A&M Athletics (2012), Texas A&M made the decision to move because the SEC would offer "national visibility, greater financial opportunity, and conference stability." In short, Texas A&M wanted to remain a part of the elite and believed moving to the SEC was the answer. However, this did not come without the associated costs of going to what has been the most dominant football conference in the 21st century.

Texas A&M: Mechanics of "Keeping Up"

The move to the SEC started to financially help Texas A&M even before they officially moved as licensing revenue increased by 24% in the first 6 months after the announcement of the move (Associated Press, 2012a). However, as ESPN contributor Sam Kahn (2012) found, with Texas A&M's move into the SEC there was also the pressure to keep up with the facilities that teams in that conference had to offer. Chris Low (2012) ranked the top SEC facilities resulting in Texas A&M being 10th out of 14. They were ranked behind teams such as Louisiana State, which had recently approved a $100 million upgrade to its stadium (Bennett, 2012); Tennessee and Arkansas, which had just opened up $45 million and $35 million football facilities (Low, 2012); and Georgia, which pumped $40 million worth of upgrades into its football facilities. Therefore, Texas A&M, which already boasted state-of-the-art facilities before the move, decided to build a new $9 million workout facility complete with all of the best equipment. Khan (2012) relayed that the facility includes:

> 16 platforms [that] serve as the centerpiece. On each of those platforms, cutting-edge technology is installed in the form of a camera system and an attached tablet where players can sign in with their names and have their workouts recorded for evaluation by Jackson and his staff. The cameras yield data from a player's lift, such as the speed of the lift and how it compares to that player's best lift. All that data can be viewed on the tablet and the video can even be accessed. (para. 7)

However, the workout facility was just the first upgrade for Texas A&M. Over 2013, 2014, and 2015 Texas A&M has been undergoing a major "Kyle Field Redevelopment" totaling $450 million (Texas A&M Athletics, 2013b). Renovations include a new west campus workout facility, a northeast tower, eastside press box and canopy, north end zone façade, new ramps, new suites, loge boxes, 12th Man Club, westside plaza, and a south end zone complex. The new construction will bring the seating capacity from 82,600 to 102,512 (Redevelopment of Kyle Field, 2014). These investments were deemed necessary to be a part of the SEC and benefit primarily football, as is often the case. As Veblen (1901/2007) or Sen (1983) might suggest, Texas A&M wanted what the elite had. And, in this case, they were able to acquire it.

The movement of Texas A&M to the SEC is expected to provide financial stability, as previously noted. The current $20 million per year given to each school is expected to substantially increase as each member is expected to receive $35 million per year just from the SEC Network once the network reaches full distribution (Bromberg, 2014). The newest television network would eventually allow the SEC to eclipse the Big 10, which has a new contract projected to pay each school roughly $45 million per year (Fornelli, 2014). Yet, the question remains: what will be the result of the continually increasing revenues? Who benefits? And what is the role of the student-athlete?

College Athletics Labor Market

An athletics department is made up of many different individuals working together to make sure the department operates appropriately. Additionally, college athletics, as outlined previously, is deeply influenced by outside sources such as network executives, governing bodies (NCAA, conference commissioners), and sponsors. For simplicity, we consider here only administrations made up of people who do get paid (i.e., athletics directors, assistant athletics directors, marketing, ticket sales, athletic academics, trainers, equipment managers, operations, communications, etc.) along with sponsors and executives as the capitalists—those making the capital investments expecting to return a profit—in juxtaposition to the student-athlete. Because it seems fairly acceptable to assume that those working in administration or executives for media and corporations are paid for their labor, we focus primarily on the student-athlete as laborer.

In order to understand the student-athlete as laborer in the labor market and how that affects competitions, we have to understand the role of the student-athlete in keeping up. Thus, we begin by first considering that the athlete is a commodity traded and sold by the capitalist. Marx (1976) noted that the commodity is made up of both a qualitative (use value) and a quantitative (value or exchange value) aspect. Use value is simply how useful a commodity is to an individual. The understanding of usefulness in a commodity is tied up in social and historical knowledge of how a commodity can be used. For example, a coat has a use value insofar as it keeps an individual warm and the individual knows that the coat can keep him or her warm because he or she has come to know this from social and historical relationships with both a coat and the cold (the student-athlete is valuable for what he or she provides to the university and its affiliated fans and sponsors). Exchange value is the exchange of one use value for another use value of the same value. Exchange value, then, is what one is willing to give up for said coat (at the current moment universities are willing to give up scholarships to student-athletes). In theory, without the existence of labor, one coat would be equal to the amount of material expended to make the coat (Harvey, 2006). Regardless, in the art of exchange, one must believe that he or she is exchanging one commodity for another of the same use value. Simply put, exchange must always be equal.

Labor is necessary for the development of surplus value (money that can be either invested or reinvested) in the creation of a commodity. Labor value is the aspect of the commodity that can make use value have a value (Marx, 1976). So the labor and labor time expended in changing the wool into a coat is what gives the coat potential surplus value. That is, labor provides the possibility of having value. This of course is just potential value. Until the labor value is valorized through the act of exchange, the commodity is not a commodity at all. When confronted in the market, the laborer decides what he or she is willing to accept for his or her labor based upon the socially agreed-upon value of labor (again, scholarship is the current compensation). Yet, the individual capitalist is not confronted directly with the labor but rather with the laborer holding the potential for labor (there is no guarantee that a student-athlete will produce any return). It is something that will ideally come to fruition later, but the laborer agrees to labor before the laborer receives the agreed-upon monetary amount (student-athletes sign and agree to give labor before receiving any scholarship). When the laborer gives him or herself to the capitalist, he or she is no longer in control of what he or she as laborer does with his or her time. Thus, the capitalist in theory is free to do what he or she wishes and will try to create the most surplus value as possible. This is the idea of exploiting the laborer (getting more out of the laborer than the value provided to the laborer; Marx, 1976).

The existence of the laborer in the market is more complicated than a typical commodity and especially so in modern society, given the fact that many of the fields in modern society are not based on production of "heavy" commodities (i.e., ships, planes, etc.) but instead "light" commodities (i.e., money; Ritzer, 2011). When extended to college athletics, the high school athlete enters the market knowing that his or her labor is worth a 1-year renewable scholarship for up to four seasons of participating in the sport of his or her choice within a 5-year span. They exchange their labor to the university and its associated sponsors for an education, in theory. The individual athlete is not allowed to capitalize on his or her talent, but the university and its associates are given permission to exploit the laborers' labor (again, we assign no social or cultural value to the term "exploit" other than the fact that the capitalist gaining surplus value from the laborers work is by definition exploitation). This agreement is the current social value for the labor of the student athlete. In this instance, the NCAA and its affiliated universities determine the social value of the student athlete as laborer in the labor market. Thus, they decree extensive boundaries upon the acts of the laborer in the form of the NCAA manual.

Student athletes are bound by the rules of the NCAA manual. The overseeing of an individual potential student-athlete begins when the person is only a freshman in high school. As indicated in Chapter 13 of the manual (NCAA, 2014f), recruiting is:

> *Any solicitation of a prospective student-athlete or a prospective student athlete's relatives (or legal guardians) by an institutional staff member or by a representative of the institution's athletics interests for the purpose of securing the prospective student-athlete's enrollment and ultimate participation in the institution's intercollegiate athletics program. (p. 89)*

The protection of the athlete and the competitive balance of the NCAA member schools are said to be at the top of the priority list. However, beginning with the recruiting of student-athletes, markets between capitalists exist.

Markets are created within this relationship of recruiting by multiple websites and recruiting services. These websites, such as Rivals, ESPN, 247, among others provide insights to customers—for a fee—into the recruiting world of every major college program. Capitalizing on exploiting the laborer, who in this instance does not agree to be in the labor market, these websites actually offer nothing to the laborer but a chance to be exposed on a national level to many wondering eyes and coaches; no recruit is paid by the site. These sites produce information, relaying information provided by others and accepting money for disseminating the information to people who pay for access to a given recruiting website. In this instance, the organization creates surplus value by fees and creating a large base of people willing to click on their site. Thus, the viewer of the website acts as laborer/commodity to be traded and sold to advertising companies (Mosco, 2009). The point here is that the capitalist exploits the laborer, both student-athlete and viewer, without providing the laborer with any monetary compensation.

One prominent example of what we are describing taken to the extreme and actually in violation of NCAA rules was Will Lyles and his online recruiting service, Complete Scouting Services. Mr. Lyles illegally accepted money from the University of Oregon to steer student-athletes toward Oregon (Smith, 2011). Particularly, Lyles was found to be intimately involved with the successful recruitment of high school all-American running back Lache Seastrunk and eventual Heisman Trophy finalist LaMichael James. Lyles initially maintained that he simply provided profiles to the coaches. However, after a 6-month investigation, Lyles admitted to the NCAA, "I look back at it now and they paid for what they saw as my access and influence with recruits" (cited by Smith, 2011). In this instance, the exploitation of the high school athlete by the recruiting websites that worked closely with Oregon essentially means that the relationship of the student-athlete as laborer for the university and its partners started before the exchange occurred in the labor market, before the athletes agreed to go to Oregon. Again, within this act, the student-athlete is not the one compensated.

Within the rulebook, the NCAA mandates that student-athletes are not permitted to accept monetary compensation for their labor, but corporate sponsors, the university, recruiting websites, and apparel companies may profit from the student-athlete (NCAA, 2014f). Essentially, once the student-athlete has given up his or her labor, he or she is in the control of the administrators and exchanged for media contracts, apparel contracts, and booster support. Simultaneously, viewers are exploited by media entities that have created free laborers out of cable contract and advertising agreements (Mosco, 2009). That is, television networks trade off of viewers. Thus, both the athlete is exploited to create surplus value for the university and the viewer is exploited by network executives and sold to advertisers so that the networks can recoup the investments made to the universities through conference television rights fees. The administrators and executives themselves hold only the potential for value, but no value in and of themselves. As Veblen (1904/2005) would suggest, they are merely cogs in the wheel of business because the athlete and sponsors cannot talk directly. Making themselves necessary means that these entities, administrators and executives, can control the actions and movements of the laborers.

In Chapter 12 of the NCAA manual, the rules are provided so that corporate entities may profit from events, professional organizations can supply money to universities (not athletes), and "promotional items (e.g., posters, postcards, film, videotapes) bearing the name or picture of a student-athlete and related to these events may be sold or distributed by the national or international sports governing body sponsoring these events or its designated third-party distributors" (NCAA, 2014f, pp. 70–71). After the student enters the university, he or she must give up any control of his or her image and ability to profit. A very relevant example of exactly what the NCAA manual dictates, and the universities helped create, can be witnessed with 2012 Heisman Trophy winner Johnny Manziel from Texas A&M university. The Heisman Trophy and the endorsements that go along with the prestigious award are quite lucrative. However, Johnny Manziel himself was not able to capitalize on his own labor, under NCAA rules, that is.

Who Owns "Johnny Football"?

Johnny Manziel was a highly touted high school football star in Texas (Texas A&M Athletics, 2013a). Johnny had multiple offers but decided to go to Texas A&M over teams such as Stanford and Oregon. Although he redshirted his freshman year in 2011, and despite being arrested shortly before the start of the 2012 season (Associated Press, 2012b), during the 2012 season, Johnny quickly took the college football world by storm, becoming the first freshman ever to win the Heisman Trophy, the most coveted individual accolade in college football. During the season, Johnny Manziel quickly became known as "Johnny Football." Importantly, Johnny Manziel comes from a well-off family due in part to a history of success in the oil industry (San Antonio Express-News, 2014). Therefore, they were aware of the potential for the university and other entities to make money from the Johnny Football moniker. In response to this understanding, Manziel set up JMan2 Enterprise LLC and trademarked "Johnny Football" in the winter of 2013 after initially being turned down for a trademark in November 2013 (Christian, 2014).

Johnny Manziel could not profit from the sale of "Johnny Football" merchandise directly because of NCAA rules. However, he could indirectly collect retribution through lawsuits. Before JMan2 successfully received the rights to "Johnny Football," numerous outlets attempted to sell T-shirts related to "Johnny Football" (Duffy, 2013a). Therefore, JMan2 sued these places for copyright infringement. Although they settled suits against two T-shirt manufacturers, Johnny was not allowed to have any of that money until he was done playing football at Texas A&M (Duffy, 2013a). Although Manziel could not profit from himself while a college athlete, Darren Rovell (2012) offered insight as to who can profit from "Johnny Football." Rovell (2012) noted that the winning of the Heisman Trophy means there is a lot of money to be made for those who have a vested interest in Texas A&M football. The only people associated with the program who cannot make money are the student-athletes, namely Manziel. As Rovell (2012) notes in his ESPN.com article:

> *Because of NCAA rules, it's an incredibly complicated business as to who is allowed to cash in and how they're allowed to make money off a player. Texas A&M can make money off Manziel by selling jerseys, T-shirts and hats with No. 2 on them, but they're not allowed to use Manziel's name, likeness or Johnny Football nickname, which was bestowed on him when he arrived in College Station. (para. 7–8)*

It was not only during this year that he quickly rose to stardom for his flashy style but he soon became famous for his off-the-field activities.

Disregarding the highly publicized off-field issues with an underage Johnny Manziel partying at nightclubs (Rauch, 2013), the problems associated with his role as student-athlete stemmed largely from the allegations that Johnny Manziel accepted money for signing memorabilia for fans (Rovell & Gubar, 2013). These charges were met with an in-depth investigation that resulted in no suspension but do point to who can benefit from the student-athlete. Rovell and Gubar (2013) noted:

> *The value of Manziel is clear in the memorabilia and appearance market: Independent merchandiser Aggieland Outfitters recently auctioned off six helmets signed by Manziel and Texas A&M's other Heisman Trophy winner, John David Crow, for $81,000. Texas A&M's booster organization, the 12th Man Foundation, sold a table for six, where Manziel and Crow will sit at the team's Kickoff Dinner later this month, for $20,000. (para. 16)*

This exploitation of the student-athlete is viewed as important and necessary for athletics departments and universities that increasingly rely on nongovernment monies to survive. It is estimated by Joyce Julius & Associates that in 2012 alone, Johnny Manziel accounted for $37 million worth of media exposure for Texas A&M (Duffy, 2013b).

This is evident in the recent discussion around the expansion of the stadium deemed necessary for Texas A&M to keep up in the SEC (Low, 2012). Although there is some disagreement between individual stakeholders on what was the driving force for raising the necessary $450 million, Texas A&M regent, Jim Schwertner, has proposed that the expanded stadium be renamed "Kyle Field: The House that Johnny Built" (Schwartz, 2014). It is his belief that the university would not have been able to build the stadium without the money raised on the back of the successes of Johnny Manziel.

Conclusion

In this chapter, we built upon the ideas of the corporate university shared in the second chapter to explain how the structures of government finance affect how universities and those acting with/on behalf of the universities make decisions. As an example, we spoke specifically about Texas A&M University to explain college athletics from a political economic grounding of "keeping up," in an effort to explain the often discussed "arms race" in college athletics as part of a larger societal structure. In this instance, and indeed in many others, we see that Texas A&M wanted to keep up with the elite programs in the country. They did so by moving into the SEC and building new facilities. The student-athlete, and particularly Johnny Manziel, is treated as a commodity toward the goal of keeping up.

In addition to Johnny Football serving the corporate sponsors, because of NCAA rules, the university must take preventative measures to protect the sponsors who support the institution. For example, Texas A&M is sponsored by Adidas. Therefore, if Nike had wanted to make a Texas A&M shirt with the number 2 (Manziel's number) on it, the university would have had to actively prohibit Nike from doing so. A failure to properly police the inappropriate selling of merchandise is viewed as a lack of institutional control, which could result in large penalties for the university athletics program. Thus, what we witness here is the NCAA actively working to protect the rights of the corporation above the athlete, or university for that matter, because they must protect their brand first and foremost. Thus, the governing body in the athletics department is an appendage of the larger corporate university, which serves the sponsors and outside dollars over the student-athletes.

In short, universities act to keep themselves in the same class as the best universities and athletics departments act to keep themselves in the same class as the best athletics departments (i.e., most profitable, prestigious, etc.). Examining college athletics through political economy helps explain how the structure of university athletics departments works, who benefits, and the role of the student-athlete in this structure. The student-athlete acts as a laborer treated as commodity in order to gain investible surplus value for athletics departments, sponsors, and media entities that absolutely have to "keep up" with the competition in order to survive.

As provided in the first chapter, the way that college athletics has been systemically altered throughout its history, in line with societal changes, requires a reflection on how funding works. However, it also requires that we consider the future of college athletics. At the same time that Johnny Football became a household name, conference realignment greatly altered the landscape of major college athletics, and both corporate interests and student fees are spending money toward college athletics at an all-time high, we must reflect on the current debates, legal cases, and future implications of the funding framework.

Following the lead of the third chapter wherein we took a micro approach in using one pertinent example to explain how athletics departments attempt to keep up with one another, the fourth chapter first builds upon Veblen presenting the results of the arms race and how college athletics departments across the country are funding themselves in an attempt to "keep up." Next, we consider some of the most relevant legal cases of today—those of the use of the player's likeness for profit by the NCAA and athletics departments while athletes make zero profit and student-athlete unionization. Building upon the history of the NCAA in the first chapter, the corporate university implications laid out in the second chapter, and the political economic theory in the third chapter, in this next chapter we consider what this might mean for the future of college athletics. The arguments are being heard louder than ever and no doubt will have implications for the future of college athletics.

Emerging Debates and the Future of Athletics in Higher Education

T HE FIRST TWO CHAPTERS detailed the foundations of the current model of NCAA athletics, and the third chapter, through the specific use of Texas A&M as a case study example, demonstrated why the athletics funding crisis has grown so large. However, a discussion of the future of college athletics within the realm of higher education indicates that the status quo of funding mechanisms in college athletics is simply not built to last. Importantly, the third chapter detailed that the crux of the funding crisis lies in the mathematically impossible quest of each athletic department to keep up with the most accomplished athletic departments. By the very definition of "the best," there can be only one. Thus, athletic department officials often irrationally pour hundreds of millions of dollars into their athletic department— frequently after seeking handouts from outside entities—on the fallacy that each athletic department can be the best. As such, the "Keeping Up with the Joneses"—alternatively known as the "Arms Race"—effect takes hold, and the athletics funding crisis continues to deepen.

Through a thorough discussion of this "Arms Race" specifically within the NCAA Division I level, an exploration of the far-reaching ramifications of the "Power Five" autonomy, the possible unionization of college athletics, and the folding of the UAB football program, it is evident that there is the potential for a restructuring of the NCAA. When the NCAA did divide into three separate divisions in 1973 (Yost, 2010), Division I was designated as such in large part because of the revenue-generating power and the commercialization efforts of a specific sect of colleges and universities that wanted to be in a division with like-minded peers. While this distinction made sense at the time—and a further division into FBS, FCS, and schools without football further classifies Division I institutions—it is important to note that within each subset there are clearly "haves" and "have nots" in regard to funding and keeping up in the facilities arms race. Discussing the specific mechanisms for such a separation of powers demonstrates that while the athletics funding crisis can be evident in different ways at different colleges, it still is a ubiquitous issue across the NCAA Division I level.

Although there have been numerous efforts to bring some sort of substantial change to the distinction that student-athletes should be defined as employees and not amateurs, the Ed O'Bannon lawsuit has carried with it the greatest chance to make lasting changes on the very definition of what it means to be a NCAA Division I student-athlete. An in-depth exploration of the backgrounds and facts of this landmark case takes place in the following pages. As will be seen throughout the discussion of the Ed O'Bannon case, it uniquely represents the far-reaching ramifications on top-down measures taken by athletic departments to combat the funding crisis in intercollegiate athletics. Specific efforts by the Northwestern football team to unionize and the administrative decision to eliminate football at the University of Alabama-Birmingham further showcase the different manifestations and potential outcomes of the athletics funding crisis.

By many different measures, the NCAA model as it stands wholeheartedly attempts to make money from college athletics. Such efforts can clearly have dramatic effects on the university setting as a whole. Ultimately, the fallout from court cases such as *O'Bannon vs. the NCAA* and the unionization efforts of the NCAA will provide substantial legal foundations for potential looming changes in the power structure of the NCAA. As we have illustrated in the preceding chapters, the current model by which we fund intercollegiate athletics is heavily intertwined with university funding, corporate monies, and student fees. For the departments that generate an excess amount of revenue (the Ohio States and Alabamas of the world), it will likely be business as usual in the coming decades. However, for those institutions relying on university funding and student fees for large portions of their budget, current events suggest trouble is potentially on the horizon. In this chapter, we detail a number of recent developments that will directly affect the sustainability of the current funding model used by the majority of Division I athletic departments.

Funding the Arms Race

Among schools in conferences that make up the Bowl Championship Series, students at Rutgers University—the flagship public university of New Jersey—provided the greatest amount of support for athletics during the 2011–2012 school year. Eichelberger and Young (2012) noted when student fees and university support through tuition reallocation were combined every student at Rutgers paid more than $1,000 to support the athletic department, the most among schools in the major six BCS conferences.

In all, Rutgers athletics received more than $28 million from the university, also the most of BCS conference schools. It was the second year Rutgers has received the dubious top honor.

> *"Rutgers puts too much money into athletics at the cost of basically every other department," said Stephen Sweeney, the Democratic president of the New Jersey Senate, in an e-mail. He applauded efforts by Athletic Director Tim Pernetti to increase revenue. At the same time, he said, "the faculty, student body and the families of students who are supporting them through school simply pay too much." (Eichelberger & Young, 2012, para. 6)*

Rutgers competed in the Big East conference against schools like the University of Louisville, which generated $27 million more in revenue than Rutgers during 2011. Additionally, Rutgers generated just over $7.5 million in contributions during 2011, whereas Louisville generated more than $28 million. The gap between the two schools gets even larger when the subsidies each school received are eliminated. Based solely on athletic revenue generation, Louisville generated $46 million more than Rutgers in 2011. For two teams expected to compete for the same athletes and the same championships, that is a noticeable dollar difference. Even while collecting more than $28 million in subsidies from the university, Rutgers paid its head football coach more than $2 million a year to try and compete with the bigger and more prestigious football programs across the country. In contrast, Louisville paid head football coach Charlie Strong $1.6 million annually during this period. Similarly, Rutgers spent $102 million on a renovation to its aging football stadium (Weaver, 2011). All of these expenditures were designed to help Rutgers compete with schools that have bigger budgets, a larger fan base to generate revenue from, and greater donor bases.

The University of Cincinnati, another former member of the Big East, was also struggling to compete financially with the rest of the conference. Public subsidies of the athletic department grew by more than 33% from 2005 to 2008, the most of any BCS conference school during that time period. Even with the allocations, the school operated with a $24 million dollar deficit. Head track and field coach Bill Schnier stated Cincinnati athletics was caught up in the vicious cycle of an "arms race" where "sports have to match the pros dollar-for-dollar in salaries in facilities . . . we'll have to find more money next year, and the year after that, and the year after that. Someone has to stop the madness" (quoted in Gillum, Upton, & Berkowitz, 2010, para. 11).

The differences in revenue and fundraising between schools are not unique to the old Big East conference. As mentioned earlier, Cal-Berkeley attempted to cut five sports from its athletic program. In the same year they were cutting programs and displacing athletes and coaches, they announced the football team would play off campus during the 2010–2011 season so its own stadium could be renovated to the tune of $321 million. The project started as a privately funded endeavor with the bulk of the cost being absorbed by long-term seat licenses and naming rights deals. Three years into the fundraising effort, the department has collected $31 million in cash and $113 million in nonbinding seat agreements that will be collected over 30 years. University officials have acknowledged they likely will not reach their fundraising goal and will have to dip into university funds to complete the project (Bachman, 2012). All of this was being discussed during a time when tuition for in-state students was raised by 17% even though the university has subsidized the athletic department with $88.4 million in allocations over the last 8 years. Add in the addition of a new training facility and Cal-Berkeley was set to borrow $474 million to complete the project.

Further, Cal-Berkeley has not traditionally been a successful football program. The Bears have not played in its conference's elite championship bowl game, the Rose Bowl, since 1959, and the Bears rarely sell out their stadium. Much like Rutgers, Cal-Berkeley is competing intraconference against schools with bigger athletics budgets, like the University of Oregon. Oregon generated more than $20 million more in revenue than Cal-Berkeley and raised more than $23 million more in contributions during 2011. In order to keep up with the larger schools in the Pac-12 conference, 15% of Cal-Berkeley's athletic budget came from university allocations. Oregon relied on allocations for only 2.8% of its athletic budget (*USA Today*, 2012).

Colorado State University has also struggled to compete with larger schools in its conference, the Mountain West. President Tony Frank acknowledged the issues while arguing Colorado State *must* keep up the other schools in their conference but believed "benchmarking" was a useful way to determine how much universities should be using to fund athletics. He noted that even though Colorado State athletics received $14.4 million in public funds for athletics in 2010, they were "only" third among public schools in the Mountain West in terms of allocation support. Further, he justified the public funding by pointing out that the Mountain West "is certainly not the highest spending conference in Division I athletics" (Frank, 2011). Frank (2011) is certainly not the first or last person to use the "everyone else is doing it" argument to support the public funding of athletic departments.

It is worth looking at the revenue differences between schools in the Big 12 Conference. The University of Texas athletic department generated more than $150 million in revenue during 2011 while receiving no financial support from the university. By way of contrast, the University of Colorado generated just over $60 million in revenue while relying on allocations for more than 25% of its athletic budget. Further, Iowa State University generated a meager $48.5 million in revenue, more than $100 million less than its conference partner Texas (*USA Today*, 2012). The differences between the Big 12 schools during the 2010–2011 school year in terms of revenue and subsidy reliance can be seen in Table 3. To put the Big 12 revenues in context,

TABLE 3
Revenues and Subsidies for Public Big 12 Schools During 2010–2011

School	Total Revenues (in millions)	Percentage Subsidy
Texas	$150.2	0.0
Oklahoma	$104.3	0.0
Texas A&M	$87.2	0.0
Oklahoma State	$82.6	7.5
Kansas	$74.8	4.6
Kansas State	$69.9	4.7
Missouri	$64.1	4.2
Texas Tech	$59.5	9.7
Iowa State	$48.5	7.7

Source: Data generated from USA Today. (2012). *Sports' college athletics finances.*

Iowa State generated similar amounts of revenue as Central Florida from Conference USA ($42.7 million) and San Diego State from the Mountain West Conference ($45.2 million). The Cyclones generated $11 million less than University of Nevada-Las Vegas, another member of the Mountain West Conference ($59.5 million).

Unlike Iowa State, these schools are not expected to compete with the Texases and Oklahomas of the world who generated more than $100 million in revenue during 1 year. However, with ongoing conference realignments, schools are more commonly finding themselves in Iowa State's position: competing for players and conference championships with schools that have much larger sources of revenue. (See West Virginia's move to the Big 12 in 2012. The Mountaineers would have fallen between Missouri and Texas Tech at the bottom end of the Big 12 revenue chart.) Even athletic departments that operate with a surplus receive support from the university. Auburn University operated with a surplus of more than $12 million, yet still received $4.9 million in student fees during the 2006–2007 school year. The surplus rose to more than $19 million in 2007–2008. An athletic department spokesman stated the department was using the funding to make facility improvements, including an $86 million upgrade to the basketball arena. As evidenced, athletic departments are requiring more public funding to be successful and sustainable.

However, administrators, students, and legislators are increasingly meeting this funding schema with resistance.

O'Bannon et al. v. the NCAA and Power Five Autonomy

Although the amateurism model used by the NCAA has increasingly been a point of criticism as revenues have soared for everyone but the players, one court case has been credited with bringing the debate over amateurism into the public conversation. In July 2009, former University of California, Los Angeles (UCLA) basketball player Ed O'Bannon filed a lawsuit on behalf of former (and eventually current) student-athletes against the NCAA (and other entities involved in business dealings with the NCAA) over the use of athletes' images by the NCAA without compensation for the athlete (Frontline, 2011). In 2014, Judge Claudia Wilken delivered what FOX Sports writer Stewart Mandel (2014) called "a decisive and crushing end to the era of amateurism in college athletics and in doing so, opened the door for even more drastic attacks on the organization going forward" (para. 2). In her decision, Wilken struck down the justifications used by NCAA officials for not compensating student-athletes and preserving the amateur athletics model where student-athletes are not entitled to anything beyond a scholarship for their participation in intercollegiate athletics. Beginning in July 2016, schools will be allowed to allocate licensing revenue into a trust for players to retrieve after their eligibility expires. Although the implications may be minor at first, Mandel (2014) noted the consequences would be far-reaching in the years to come:

> [The] ruling only opened the door for years and years of more law-suits and perhaps even Congressional rulings. Wilken's strong words in deflating the amateurism model will become the template for thirsty lawyers smelling further NCAA blood... No one can possibly predict where this will all wind up. All we know is that on August 8, 2014, a federal judge in California sized up the testimony of [NCAA administrators] called to defend college sports' amateurism model and said—I'm not buying it. (para. 17)

In addition to the O'Bannon case, schools in the five biggest conferences (deemed the Power Five) voted to have autonomy to decide many of their own rules moving forward. For example, schools will have the option to offer "full-cost-of-attendance" scholarships that cover the expenses associated with attending college that non-student-athletes have the option to cover by working part-time jobs. The University of Connecticut estimated providing a cost of attendance allotment for all athletes on full athletic scholarships would initially cost the department between $1 million and $1.5 million dollars annually (Wilson, 2015). The fact that many schools (the University of Texas and University of Nebraska, to name two) have already stated they will offer full-cost-of-attendance scholarships indicates this will no longer be "optional" if universities want to compete with the other schools in their conference when recruiting student-athletes. For example, Rutgers University is in the same conference, the Big Ten, as the University of Nebraska and would seemingly be at a recruiting disadvantage if they do not offer full-cost-of-attendance scholarships.

For schools like Rutgers that rely heavily on subsidies to balance their budget, the O'Bannon ruling (and subsequent rulings) and Power Five autonomy will only complicate matters. In 2013, Rutgers' largest source of revenue was rights and licensing fees of more than $13 million. If that revenue were directly shared with the players, the university would have to reduce expenses or rely even more heavily on student fees and university funding to survive (Rutgers relied on more than $45 million in student fees and school funds to survive in 2013; Berkowitz et al., 2014). In all, the O'Bannon ruling and Power Five autonomy will only add to the expenses associated with operating an athletic department in the years to come. Many have posited these developments will cause the most (financially) successful programs to get richer, whereas lesser programs will be forced to make hard choices in regard to their athletic programs. As Ivan Maisel (2014) of ESPN surmised after the autonomy vote, "on this day, the NCAA voted that the strong shall inherit the earth . . . this is the haves saying to the have-nots, 'enough already'" (para. 1–2).

Leaders at San Jose State University (SJSU)—a school not in a Power Five Conference—have indicated that its 2015–2016 operating budget will include an additional $1.6 million to be allocated to cover the increased costs associated with funding full cost-of-attendance scholarships. In their budget update, SJSU asserts that this funding measure is in order to be "consistent with all schools in the Mountain West Conference and the other NCAA Division I Bowl Subdivision conferences" (Harris, 2015, para. 8). Such examples at Rutgers and SJSU point to the notion that the new cost-of-attendance legislation could increase and has increased subsidies given to athletics.

The Unionization of College Athletes

Although these top-down measures will certainly influence the funding of intercollegiate athletics, a small group of athletes at Northwestern University are also aiming to change the college sport dynamic. In January 2014, the president of the National College Players Association filed for unionization rights on behalf of Northwestern football players with the National Labor Relations Board (NLRB). On March 26 of the same year, the NLRB ruled the scholarship football players are considered employees and orders an election to take place. As of December 2014, the appeal filed by Northwestern University is still being considered. If the appeal is unsuccessful, the votes cast by 76 football players will be counted and Northwestern football could become the first player union in intercollegiate sports. At private schools similar to Northwestern (Notre Dame and Vanderbilt to name a few), student-athletes could form similar unions and negotiate benefits, scholarships, and other governance issues with the university (Vint, 2014).

Mark Emmert, the embattled NCAA president, asserted that allowing intercollegiate athletes to unionize would fundamentally alter the landscape of all that is good and pure about the NCAA. Furthermore, he has addressed the perception between university funding and revenue generated by the potential revenue-generating sports of football and men's basketball. In an interview aired on CBS during programming for the 2014 NCAA Men's Basketball Tournament, Emmert stated:

> The billions of dollars that come in, and it is a very large amount of money that universities receive for intercollegiate athletics in two sports, football and basketball, that also is what drives and pays for

all of the other expenses in intercollegiate athletics. So track and field, soccer, women's volleyball, women's basketball ... all of those sports are paid for by the revenue that comes in from two sports that drive all of that activity. So the notion that somehow universities are taking that money and putting it in the bank is utterly erroneous. They're using it to pay for nearly half a million student-athletes. (Femia, 2014, para. 4)

Although it may seem far-fetched currently, a cursory look at other collectively bargained agreements between athletes and leagues could be used as a base for college agreements. In the National Basketball Association, players are entitled to 51.5% of the revenue generated (Coon, 2011). In the National Football League, players receive between 40% and 55% of revenue streams (Ejiochi, 2014). Arrangements similar to this could do great damage to the department financing as Northwestern football generates approximately $30 million annually for the athletic department and subsidizes many of the other sports at Northwestern that operate in the red (Curry, 2014). Further, commentators have argued health care, litigation, and discrimination costs could also skyrocket. As Fowler (2014) stated:

[Private schools] could incur serious expenses to fulfill player needs under a union model. Operating within the NCAA's rigid amateurism rules would become increasingly difficult for several reasons, two neutral experts say: state/federal labor laws, the threat of having to pay players a minimum wage salary, increased chance of discrimination lawsuits and the College Athletes Players Association's desire to allow commercial compensation for athletes. (para. 8)

Additionally, public universities may also be affected. If Northwestern football players are set to receive a cut of the revenue, they would have a distinct advantage over their public counterparts. The NCAA would also be forced to consider additional rule changes to level the playing field between the public and private institutions. In almost all of these scenarios, athletic departments would be maintaining less of the revenue generated. Brian Phillips (2014) of Grantland succinctly described the stakes of the decision:

> *Short of congressional legislation, which is not going to happen, can you think of anything that could change the system faster than the threat of the players refusing to play? A union would give players two things they currently lack: a mechanism to negotiate their own deals and leverage to exact concessions from their employers. It's how the pros do it, and it's the only solution I've seen that doesn't depend on administrators just arbitrarily deciding to be less greedy. (para. 22)*

The Elimination of UAB Football

One potential consequence of decreased revenue for athletic departments is the cutting of established sport programs. The University of Alabama-Birmingham (UAB) announcement in early December 2014 that the football team would be shut down at the end of the 2014 season was met with disappointment and backlash, but the announcement did not come as a surprise to those who closely followed the program (Evans, 2014). The final announcement came at the conclusion of a yearlong, campus-wide strategic planning process studying the financial health and viability of more than 10 university departments (Barrabi, 2014; Evans, 2014; Solomon, 2014).

Several signs pointed to the imminent demise of the football program. Chiefly, the contract of the successful head football coach was not extended, and no nonconference opponents were scheduled past the 2016 season (Evans, 2014). In an era in which successful coaches are offered contract extensions to provide security to the athletic department and nonconference opponents are often scheduled 5 or 6 years in advance, there were telltale signs of UAB President Ray Watts's announcement regarding the UAB football program.

Although Watts's justification for cutting the program was almost purely financial, pundits (a) argued cutting the program causes a bleaker financial future for the athletic department as a whole (Solomon, 2014) and (b) insisted political maneuvers on the University of Alabama System Board of

Trustees pushed for the termination of the UAB football program (Barrabi, 2014; Davis, 2015; Evans, 2014).

By no longer serving as a football member of Conference USA, UAB "is projected to lose roughly $2 million per year in NCAA and Conference USA revenue starting in 2015–16" (Solomon, 2014, para. 45), money that would have been from C-USA TV money for football games, the College Football Playoff, and bowl game payouts. Furthermore, there is no guarantee that UAB will even continue to be a member of Conference USA because conference by-laws require its members to field a football team (Solomon, 2014). Although it is true that UAB was not one of the 20 or so NCAA FBS athletic departments that have expenses that exceed revenue (Barrabi, 2014), it could be argued that cutting the program at UAB—and missing out on football contractual payouts—may cause the proverbial sinking ship to sink even faster.

Finally, supporters of the UAB football program continue to insist that the University of Alabama System Board of Trustees largely swayed Watts's decision to cut the UAB football program because of the push for the board to largely favor the University of Alabama and its Crimson Tide football program (Barrabi, 2014; Davis, 2015; Evans, 2014). Reasons differ for reasons behind this favoritism shown toward the Tuscaloosa flagship school—feuds with a former UAB athletic director, threats of a successful UAB football program that could rival the University of Alabama, and ill will between the legendary Bear Bryant family and UAB—but Watts and the board have denied any sort of misguided behind-the-scenes maneuvers to dissolve the UAB football program. After all these critiques came to light through traditional and social media, the program was restored for the 2016 season. However, the majority of the players, and even the head coach, had moved on to other opportunities before this announcement.

In all, if resources become more scarce, turf wars for university and legislative funding for athletics will only increase. Additionally, athletic administrators may have to decide the ultimate value of fielding traditionally expensive sports if support, financial and otherwise, from the university lessens. The events described here are just a few of the major issues currently ongoing that will have an impact on the financing of intercollegiate athletics in the coming years. The issues described will be further exacerbated if the trend of declining state support for higher education continues while athletic departments are forced to distribute greater amounts of compensation to the student-athletes.

Considering Results of New Structures

As noted several times in the preceding parts of this monograph, the college presidents, athletics directors, coaches, sponsors, etc., all greatly benefit from the current structure of the NCAA. The recent decisions by the courts have inspired many to consider ways in which college athletics could be altered. Reformers, such as Gerdy (2006), have urged leaders to consider alternative structures of the NCAA and have demanded buy-in from faculty, presidents, athletics directors, and coaches. Gerdy implores presidents to restructure the role of athletics in the university by eliminating scholarships, coaches to be involved in reform by focusing on educating themselves through advanced degrees that consider education and coaching of athletes, and ultimately for the structure to change from "the current school-based professional model to a community-based club system similar to the European model" (p. 229), wherein sports clubs exist and athletic scholarships are not given. This model, Gerdy suggested, is one that would focus on "using athletics as a tool to supplement the educational development of participants and promoting broad-based participation in activities that can be practiced for a lifetime in the interests of public health" (p. 230).

Although some have taken calls for reform seriously, instead of moving toward a community-based model, we have continually witnessed an uptick in administrators, executives, and the NCAA seeking to make more money from college athletics. This speaks to the overall shift in political economic structure in society toward a market driven state. Yet, somehow, despite clear evidence otherwise, until the Northwestern ruling, "Courts had told them (student-athletes) that they are not in a labor market" (LeRoy, 2015, p. 54). Furthermore, LeRoy suggested that the NCAA is overestimating the threat of unionization. The National Football League has twice decided to decertify their union because they did not want to collectively bargain under the National Labor Relations Act, and in 1987 during a labor stop, "The court endorsed the NFL's argument that the Sherman Act would apply, for example, if the players ceased to be represented by a union" (LeRoy, 2015, p. 50). When the union disbanded, it ended its own bargaining authority and the National Football League lost its antitrust exemption. This allowed the National Football League Players Association to negotiate for free agency and a percentage of gross revenues in 1993, and the union recertified until 2011 when they sought protection against a lockout under the Sherman Act.

Ultimately, LeRoy (2015) argues that the unionization of players is not a threat to the NCAA because, "the unionization effort by the College Athletes Players Association (CAPA) could end with a court ruling that Northwestern University football players are not employees under the NLRA. The regional director's decision conflicts with the Board's precedent in *Brown University and International Union, United Automobile, Aerospace and Agricultural Implement Workers of America, UAW AFL-CIO*" (p. 55). However, he believes that athletes could be served better by going the antitrust route because courts have historically favored players over wealthy owners. Under this protection, former athletes won the ruling against video game developers and antitrust law could be used to certify all Division I players, whereas the ruling in the Northwestern case is regional.

With so many people benefitting from college athletics and its ties to the corporate university—as elucidated by Texas A&M's Jason Cook being praised as an innovator for aligning the university brand to the athletic brand—it seems naïve to believe that the overall structure will change any time soon. However, antitrust litigation appears to hold some opportunities for the athletes to join together and, at the very least, secure health insurance, across the board guaranteed scholarships, and an overall voice in the decision making of the NCAA.

Conclusion

The overall goal of this monograph is to highlight the increasingly complex relationship between the oft-visible athletic department and the rest of the university. This chapter intentionally focused on the most hot-button, consequential recent events that could legitimately directly alter not only the structure of the NCAA itself but also the role of the athletic department within the university setting. By giving specific examples of the fledging budget at Rutgers University and the drastic reliance on subsidies from the university and then comparing Rutgers to the robust athletic department revenues at the University of Louisville, we demonstrated the clear distinction of "haves" and "have nots" even within the Power Five Conferences. Additionally, this specific example illustrated the disparity that can exist even *within* the same athletic conference. These disparities—and the dramatic financial funding measures taken by the "have nots" to attempt to remain relevant athletically—further demonstrate the mathematically flawed idea of pouring resources into athletics in order to be successful. As delineated in the third chapter, by definition, not all athletic departments can have teams that always win conference championships or always win national championships. Just as there are winners and losers on the field or on the court, there are (a few) winners and (a lot of) losers in the financial arms race that is currently inundating Division I college athletics.

An underlying issue in the athletics funding crisis is the very relevant debate of whether student-athletes should be classified as employees for their respective athletic departments and universities. From different angles, the Ed O'Bannon vs. the NCAA court case and the unionization efforts by the Northwestern football team both represent significant cases that could fundamentally alter and realistically crumble the NCAA as we know it. As it stands, athletic departments do not pay their student-athletes as employees. The athletic funding crisis is at its peak currently. Legislation and courtroom decisions that would make it so athletic departments have to pay student-athletes could be the proverbial straw that breaks the back of the NCAA. Imagine if a school like Rutgers University had to add the colossal expense of paying its student-athletes on top of already asking the university for $27 million dollars annually to offset athletic department costs.

In regard to athletics funding issues dramatically reshaping the structure of athletic departments, consider the possibility of athletic departments cutting high-profile athletic programs. When UAB cut its football program at the end of the 2014 football season, it represented a historic decision of sorts.

It was the first time such a high-profile program with the potential for revenue generation had been cut at an FBS institution in such a direct strategy to combat funding issues within the athletic department. Additionally, although proponents of the elimination of the UAB program outlined how cutting the program would save the athletic department from losing money on its football program, cutting the football program dramatically affected other revenue sources for the athletic department (i.e., money from the conference football television contract and the conference bylaw that member schools must have a football team).

Ultimately, the increasingly entangled relationship between the college athletic departments and the college as a whole exists because of the changing roles of athletics in the university setting. Also of paramount importance is the idea that athletic departments are experiencing funding crises at the same time that institutions of higher education are becoming progressively strapped for financial resources. Thus, it is not as though there is a surplus of money at the institutional level that can be given to augment athletic department budgets. As we have detailed throughout this monograph, athletic departments are experiencing growing expenses amid concerns that student-athletes could have to be paid as employees. As such, they often rely on subsidies directly from either the university or from the general student body to stay afloat financially. Thus, although the athletic department can often serve as the front porch for the university, the athletic department frequently muddies the actual foundation and infrastructure of the university as a whole.

Conclusion and Challenges for Future Research

I N THE PRECEDING CHAPTERS, we have examined a number of elements surrounding the connection between higher education and athletic departments. Our aim was to provide the audience with a broad overview of the athletics governance structure and highlight a number of ways in which the relationships between higher education, big-time college athletics, and the private sector can muddy the proverbial fiscal and social waters. Intercollegiate athletics, and the current NCAA governance model, is at a crossroads likely not seen in the long and elaborate history of the organization. We hope we have shown that the current funding model for college sports is likely not sustainable due to a combination of outside and internal forces that will eventually force major changes. Furthermore, although we think the athletic department often does serve as the "front porch" of the university, the front porch is not always clean. Based on a litany of NCAA scandals and related attempted cover-ups at the athletic department and institutional level, efforts are often made to whitewash the front porch that is the university athletic department. An in-depth discussion of the NCAA's most powerful—and arguably most egregious—scandals will further highlight the power dynamic than can sometimes exist under the NCAA governance model.

Specifically, the scandals with Florida State University (FSU) and the Tallahassee Police Department, the University of North Carolina (UNC) and academic performance, Baylor University and the cover-up attempt of a murder, and Pennsylvania State University (Penn State) and its reprehensible child sexual abuse case illustrate that athletic departments do not necessarily always serve as the ideal model for the university's institutional brand.

In a detailed commentary on improprieties with the handling of police matters regarding Florida State University athletics, *New York Times* journalists Mike McIntire and Walt Bogdanich (2014) provide a scathing critique of FSU athletics. In their piece titled "At Florida State, Football Clouds Justice," they assert, "Last year, the deeply flawed handling of a rape allegation against the quarterback Jameis Winston drew attention to institutional failures by law enforcement and Florida State officials" (McIntire & Bogdanich, 2014, para. 7). McIntire and Bogdanich align themselves with what has been articulated throughout this monograph: the well-being of the community and university can be tightly woven into the successes (and failures) of the high-profile athletic teams at the university.

In their in-depth investigation using police and court records and interviews with witnesses, they found that the Tallahassee Police Department has on "numerous occasions...soft-pedaled allegations of wrongdoing by Seminoles football players" (para. 8). They discuss specific cases involving allegations of theft, assault, and rape. While discussing how FSU athletics is woven into the university and local Tallahassee community, McIntire & Bogdanich (2014) point out that the performance goals for the FSU president "included enhancing 'the partnership' between the Boosters and the athletic department" (para. 26). Although this particular commentary focuses on their in-depth investigation of possible improprieties between FSU and the Tallahassee Police Department, the authors acknowledge the underlying issues in this case are not simply singular to FSU by cautioning, "The benefits that flow from a top-tier team, and the incentives it creates to protect the franchise, are not unique to Florida State; indeed, they can be found in college towns across the country" (McIntire & Bogdanich, 2014, para. 30).

Although the recent academic scandal at the University of North Carolina is strikingly different than the aforementioned issues at FSU, it does similarly illustrate cover-up attempts of deplorable actions. At UNC, two employees in UNC's African and Afro-American studies department headed fake classes over a span of nearly 20 years (Lyall, 2014; Mushnick, 2014). Almost half of the students who took these classes—in which students would receive credit for classes that never met, never had any assignments, and/or had one paper due at the end of the semester that was graded quite leniently— were student-athletes; 3,100 students overall (approximately 1,500 of whom were student-athletes) received credit for such "classes" (Lyall, 2014). Citing the report released by the attorney Kenneth Weinstein, Lyall (2014) said, "After skimming a student's paper, [Professor] Nyang'oro 'would then assign grades based largely on his assessment of the impact that grade would have on the student's ability to remain eligible'" (Lyall, 2014, para 14). This comprehensive report detailing the intricacies of the academic scandal was released in October of 2014. Mere weeks later, Mushnick (2014) penned an article titled "Media Already Quick to Forget UNC Academic Scandal" in which he opined that the academic endeavors of student-athletes are often pushed to the margins. Mushnick (2014) acknowledged that UNC's case was extreme but also said,

> But understand: UNC operated mere inches beyond the sustained norm of many-to-most Division I colleges. On the day a full-scholarship basketball or football recruit enters school, his time, focus and fanny belong to the athletic department, not the school part of the school. A legit education is optional, a matter of accident. (para. 5)

In an arguably even more serious case in 2003, news broke that Baylor men's basketball player Patrick Dennehy had been found dead in a field. The alleged murderer was his Baylor teammate, Carlton Dotson (Vecsey, 2005; Wise, 2003). Two years later, Dotson was sentenced to 35 years in prison for shooting Dennehy twice in the side of the head. These tragic events contained enough scandal to constitute a major NCAA crisis. The scandal became even worse when it was revealed that Baylor men's basketball coach Dave Bliss had illegally transferred significant amounts of money to Dennehy (Wise, 2003). When Bliss learned of the Dennehy murder, he assumed investigators would look into Dennehy's bank account. Fearful they would discover that he had transferred money impermissibly to Dennehy and that he would subsequently be penalized, Bliss plotted to change the story (Wise, 2003). He told his players to portray Dennehy as a drug dealer who often received large sums of money. As such, the large sums of money in Dennehy's bank account would be from drug deals and not from Coach Bliss himself (Wise, 2003).

Understandably uncomfortable with this coercive behavior, Baylor assistant men's basketball coach Abar Rouse secretly recorded Bliss telling his players to lie to investigators about Dennehy's drug-dealing background (Moore, 2005). Bliss was forced to resign along with the athletic director and all coaches, managers, and administrative assistants in the men's basketball offices (Moore, 2005; Wise, 2003). Under NCAA sanctions, Baylor was limited to giving 9 of a possible 14 athletic scholarships each year for the 2003–2004 and 2004–2005 seasons (Moore, 2005). Out of college coaching since he resigned in 2003, Bliss was hired as the head men's basketball coach at Southwestern Christian University in Bethany, Oklahoma in April 2015 (Khurshudyan, 2015). After news of the hire, Rob Dauster, a senior writer for NBC sports tweeted "Dave Bliss painted a player that was MURDERED as a drug dealer to hide the fact he was illegally funding his scholarship" (Khurshudyan, 2015, para. 4).

Finally, on November 5, 2011, former Penn State University assistant football coach Jerry Sandusky was arrested on 40 counts of sexually abusing eight boys over a 15-year period (Sablich, Fessenden, & McLean, 2012). Two days later, athletic director Tim Curley and Penn State vice president Gary Schutz resigned. On November 9, 2011, the board of trustees fired head coach Joe Paterno and university president Graham Spanier. Reports of sexual abuse by Sandusky date back to as early as 1998, and evidence points to cover-up efforts by university administrators and Paterno (Jones, 2015; Sablich et al., 2012; Schwartz, 2015). Until he died in January 2012, Paterno maintained he did not know the extent of the instances of sexual abuse committed by Sandusky. On June 22, 2012, Sandusky was found guilty of sexually abusing 10 boys and of 45 of the 48 counts against him. He was later sentenced to 30–60 years in prison (Jones, 2015). In July 2012, the NCAA fined Penn State $60 million, instituted a postseason ban for 4 years, took away four scholarships per year, and vacated all 112 of Penn State's wins since 1998 (Jones, 2015; Sablich et al., 2012). In early January 2015, the NCAA reached a deal with Penn State to reverse some of these aforementioned NCAA sanctions.

Most notably, the 112 wins were restored (111 of which were credited to Paterno, making him again the winningest coach in NCAA Division I football history), scholarship and postseason limitations were lifted, and the $60 million in fines would go to help fund in-state child abuse programs in Pennsylvania (Brady, Axon, & Berkowitz, 2015; Jones, 2015).

Amid a combination of support for and bewilderment at the NCAA's deal to reverse sanctions, CNN's Roxanne Jones (2015) and ESPN's Keith Olbermann (Schwartz, 2015) published scathing criticisms of the NCAA, Penn State, and Penn State athletics. Jones was a founding editor of *ESPN The Magazine* and a former vice president at ESPN. She is also an alumna of Penn State. In her CNN column titled "Penn State Still Doesn't Get It" (2015) that she wrote shortly after the NCAA's restoration of 112 Penn State victories, she professed:

> *We've [Penn State has] cheated the system, bullied our way back into the record books. And we've told the world once again that in Happy Valley winning is more important than anything. All those boys who were raped? Well, that's not our problem. What's important is making sure Coach Paterno's 409-136-3 is restored. … He was not an honorable man—not when it came to putting the lives and safety of children above football. And no NCAA ruling can change that history. (para. 13, para. 21)*

ESPN's Keith Olbermann shared similar sentiments on his televised show on ESPN on January 16, 2015, when he succinctly summed up his opinion by saying:

> *It is hard to believe that the NCAA and the school could take the most nauseating, the most horrifying, the most indefensible institutionalization of corruption in American sports—the Jerry Sandusky scandal—and make it worse, but today they just did. (Schwartz, 2015, para. 5)*

Ultimately, these examples serve to illustrate that although NCAA Division I athletic departments frequently serve as the most visible faction of a university, they do not always cast the university in a positive light. Just as the front porch is often what first draws attention to a house, university athletic departments often first draw in those in external constituency groups (fans, corporate sponsors, students, prospective students, etc.). Scandals at Florida State University, the University of North Carolina, Baylor University, and Penn State University emphatically show that athletic department personnel and university officials often hasten to continually remake the proverbial front porch in order to promote the image of the athletic department and the university. However, history has shown that when these cover-ups are revealed, the image of the entire university can take a hit.

Another challenge worth mentioning is that it is also quite difficult to isolate the most accurate revenues and expenses in intercollegiate athletics. On the revenue side, many universities count subsidies and student fees as revenue even though the athletic department played no part in earning them. Further, expenses are sometimes inflated by gold plating where administrators spend down excess revenues on amenities and salaries that are not essential to the operation of the athletic department. Hruby (2013) detailed the often excessive salaries and bonuses paid to athletic administrators, noting that,

> At Kansas State, AD John Currie's contract stipulates that any time a Wildcats head coach earns a performance bonus, he receives a bonus equal to 75 percent of the money paid to the coach, even though Currie does no actual coaching. At Louisville, [athletic director Tom] Jurich even has a contractual clause that requires him to be paid more than $250,000 in severance if he's fired for breaking NCAA rules or other misconduct. (para. 12)

Thus, we hope future researchers and commentators will note the fuzzy accounting that often takes place and highlight the inaccuracies in the popular narratives on both sides of the amateurism and athletic funding debates.

We also will be quite interested in how athletes in nonrevenue sports are affected by the changing NCAA landscape. One advantage of the current top-heavy NCAA revenue structure is the opportunities provided to athletes in sports like tennis, golf, rowing, and other lesser known sports. Although the motives for sponsoring these sports may not be the most genuine, athletes are still able to continue their athletic pursuits in a competitive and structured environment. The extent to which revenue distribution would affect these opportunities is of great interest to us and, it is hoped, will be explored throughout the changes happening in intercollegiate athletics.

Finally, we challenge future researchers to examine these upcoming changes longitudinally. One major area that is lacking in the research is examinations of the governance changes as they happen. Restated, we hope scholars will track the financial and social implications of events like student-athlete unionization in real time instead of cursory examinations after reform has set in. As previous research has shown, the immediate and lasting impacts are often quite different and immense value can come from noting the discourse and facts at both points in time. With NCAA reform discussions, the rhetoric surrounding potential changes is as strong or stronger than when actual change happens as we saw in the O'Bannon case. As Chris DuFresne (2014) of the *Los Angeles Times* noted, a litany of questions must be considered when discussing NCAA reform: "Will [a] stipend cover athletes in all sports? What about those on partial scholarships? And what about Title IX, the landmark federal decision that demands equality for female athletes? 'The devil is in the details,' said Dan Guerrero, UCLA's athletic director" (para. 20).

References

Abraham, Z. (2011, February 10). "Save Cal Sports?" Does the University of California care? *The San Francisco Chronicle*. Retrieved from http://blog.sfgate.com/abraham/2011/02/10/save-cal-sports-does-the-university-of-california-care/

Anderson, P. M. (2012). Title IX at forty: An introduction and historical review of forty legal developments that shaped gender equity law. *Marquette Sports Law Review, 22*(325), 1–55.

Associated Press. (2012a, June 30). Texas A&M officially joins SEC on Sunday, but move already paying off for Aggies. Retrieved from http://www.al.com/sports/index.ssf/2012/06/texas_am_officially_joins_sec.html

Associated Press. (2012b, June 29). A&M QB Johnny Manziel arrested. Retrieved from http://espn.go.com/college-football/story/_/id/8112673/texas-aggies-freshman-qb-johnny-manziel-arrested

Bachman, R. (2012, April). Cal's Football-Stadium Gamble. *The Wall Street Journal*. Retrieved from http://www.wsj.com/articles/SB10001424052702304432704577350214257041598

Barrabi, T. (2014, December 10). UAB football cancellation could become trend amid concern over NCAA student-athlete compensation suit. *International Business Times*. Retrieved from http://www.ibtimes.com/uab-football-cancellation-could-become-trend-amid-concern-over-ncaa-student-athlete-1734323

Bass, J. R., & Newman, J. I. (2013). Too big to fail: The Penn State scandal and the crisis of the corporate university [Special issue]. *Journal of Issues in Intercollegiate Athletics*, 22–40.

Benedict, J., & Keteyian, A. (2013). *The system: The glory and scandal of big-time college football*. New York, NY: Doubleday.

Benford, R. (2007). The college sports reform movement: Reframing the "edutainment" industry. *The Sociological Quarterly, 48*(1), 1–28.

Bennett, B. (2012, June 14). Arms race proves recession-proof. *ESPN*. Retrieved from http://espn.go.com/college-football/story/_/id/8047787/college-football-facilities-arms-race-proves-recession-proof

Berkowitz, S., Schnaars, C., Upton, J., Moran, M., Angell, J., Mangum, E., . . . Taylor, R. (2014). College finances. *USA Today*. Retrieved from http://www.usatoday.com/sports/college/schools/finances/

Berkowitz, S., Upton, J., McCarthy, M., & Gillum, J. (2010, October). How student fees boost college sports amid rising budgets. *USA Today*. Retrieved from http://www.usatoday.com/sports/college/2010-09-21-student-fees-boost-college-sports_N.htm

Blackford, L. (2012, April 1). College sports come at a cost to Kentucky taxpayers. *The Lexington Herald-Leader*. Retrieved from http://www.kentucky.com/2012/04/01/2134910/college-sports-come-at-a-cost.html

Bok, D. (2003). *Universities in the marketplace*. Princeton, NJ: Princeton University Press.

Brady, E., Axon, R., & Berkowitz, S. (2015, January 16). With Penn State wins restored, Joe Paterno the winningest coach again. *USA Today*. Retrieved from http://www.usatoday.com/story/sports/ncaaf/bigten/2015/01/16/ncaa-joe-paterno-wins-restored-penn-state-settlement/21867685/

Branch, T. (2011, October). The shame of college athletics. *The Atlantic*. Retrieved from http://www.theatlantic.com/magazine/archive/2011/10/the-shame-of-college-sports/8643

Bromberg, N. (2014, May 30). SEC network could be worth over $35 million for each conference school. *Yahoo! Sports*. Retrieved from http://sports.yahoo.com/blogs/ncaaf-dr-saturday/sec-network-could-be-worth-over--35-million-for-each-conference-school-152409523.html?pt=Array2012-08-04.html

BTN: Big Ten Network. (2014). About us. Retrieved from http://btn.com/about/

Byers, W., & Hammer, C. (1995). *Unsportsmanlike conduct: Exploiting college athletes*. Ann Arbor: The University of Michigan Press.

Carlton, C. (2010, June 12). Pac-10 commish flying to Texas, Oklahoma to invite. *Dallas Morning News*. Retrieved from http://www.dallasnews.com/sports/college-sports/texas-longhorns/20100611-Pac-10-commish-flying-to-Texas-584.ece

Christian, C. (2014, May 13). Manziel enters NFL with an end to legal fight over "Johnny Football" name. *The Chronicle*. Retrieved from http://www.chron.com/news/houston-texas/texas/article/Manziel-enters-NFL-with-an-end-to-legal-fight-5474259.php

Clotfelter, C. T. (2011). *Big-time sports in American universities*. New York, NY: Cambridge University Press.

Coon, L. (2011, November 28). Breaking down changes in new CBA. *ESPN*. Retrieved from http://espn.go.com/nba/story/_/page/CBA-111128/how-new-nba-deal-compares-last-one

Copeland, J. (2007, August 27). Moratorium lets Division 1 pause to ponder growth. *The NCAA News*. Retrieved from http://fs.ncaa.org/Docs/NCAANewsArchive/2007/Division+I/moratorium%2Blets%2Bdivision%2Bi%2Bpause%2Bto%2Bponder%2Bgrowth%2B-%2B08-27-07%2B-%2Bncaa%2Bnews.html

Crosby, F. J. (1982). *Relative deprivation and working women*. New York: Oxford University Press.

Cummings, S. (1988). *Business elites and urban development: Case studies and critical perspectives*. Albany: State University of New York Press.

Curry, C. (2014, April 25). What unionizing athletes would mean for college sports. *ABC News*. Retrieved from http://abcnews.go.com/US/unionizing-athletes-college-sports/story?id=23469250

Davis, B. (2015, February 2). Bell: UAB, Birmingham would benefit from separate board. *Birmingham Business Journal*. Retrieved from http://www.bizjournals.com/birmingham/news/2015/02/02/bell-uab-birmingham-would-benefit-from-separate.html

Denhart, M., & Vedder, R. (2010). *Intercollegiate athletics subsidies.* Washington, DC: Center for College Affordability and Productivity. Retrieved from http://www.centerfor collegeaffordability.org/uploads/ICA_Subsidies_RegressiveTax.pdf

Dent, M. (2012, August 26). Television is the ruling body of college sports. *Pittsburgh Post-Gazette.* Retrieved from http://www.post-gazette.com/stories/sports/college-national/ television-is-the-ruling-body-of-college-sports-650506/

Drape, J. (2010, September 28). Cal-Berkeley cuts 5 athletic programs. *The New York Times.* Retrieved from http://www.nytimes.com/2010/09/29/sports/29cal.html

Duderstadt, J. J. (2009). *Intercollegiate athletics and the American university: A university president's perspective.* Ann Arbor: University of Michigan Press.

Duffy, T. (2013a, February 25). Johnny Manziel trademarked "Johnny Football," can profit from T-shirt lawsuit. *The Big Lead.* Retrieved from http://thebiglead.com/2013/ 02/25/250743/

Duffy, T. (2013b, January 18). Johnny Manziel Heisman run generated $37 million in media exposure for Texas A&M. *The Big Lead.* Retrieved from http://thebiglead.com/ 2013/01/18/johnny-manziel-heisman-run-generated-37-million-in-media-exposure-for -texas-am/

Dufresne, C. (2014, June 3). College sports' billion-dollar issue: Who pays freight on pay-to-play? *Los Angeles Times.* Retrieved from http://www.latimes.com/sports/la-sp-ncaa -problems-dufresne-20140604-column.html#page=1

Eder, S., & Strauss, B. (2014, June 9). Understanding Ed O'Bannon's suit against the N.C.A.A. *The New York Times.* Retrieved from http://www.nytimes.com/2014/06/10/ sports/ncaabasketball/understanding-ed-obannons-suit-against-the-ncaa.html?_r=1

Eichelberger, C., & Young, E. (2012, May). Rutgers football fails profit test as students pay $1,000. *Bloomberg Business.* Retrieved from http://www.bloomberg.com/news/ 2012-05-03/rutgers-football-fails-profit-test-as-students-pay-1-000.html

Ejiochi, I. (2014, September 4). How the NFL makes the most money of any pro sport. *CNBC.* Retrieved from http://www.cnbc.com/id/101884818#

Evans, T. (2014, November 30). Alabama-Birmingham to fire athletic director, shut down football program. *Sports Illustrated.* Retrieved from http://www.si.com/college-football/2014/ 11/30/alabama-birmingham-shuts-down-football-program-fires-athletic-director

Femia, W. (2014, March 31). NCAA prez: Unionizing student athletes is wrong. *MSNBC.* Retrieved from http://www.msnbc.com/msnbc/ncaa-prez-mark-emmert-unionizing -student-athletes-wrong

Fornelli, T. (2014, April 26). Big Ten schools projected to make $45 million with new TV deal. *CBS Sports.* Retrieved from http://www.cbssports.com/collegefootball/eye-on-college -football/24540002/big-ten-schools-projected-to-get-45-million-with-new-tv-deal

Foundation for Individual Rights in Education. (2012). *A brief history of mandatory student fees.* Retrieved from http://thefire.org/public/pdfs/student-fees-2.pdf?direct

Fowler, J. (2014, April 21). Players as employees? High costs of college football union is in millions. *CBS Sports.* Retrieved from http://www.cbssports.com/collegefootball/eye-on -college-football/24534813/players-as-employees-looking-at-the-real-costs-of-a-college -football-union

Frank, T. (2011, December). *Athletics—Why and at what cost?* Retrieved from http://www .president.colostate.edu/speeches/athletics-december-2011.aspx

Freedberg, L. (2011, February 7). UC Berkeley asked to absorb $80M of Brown's $500m cut. *California Watch*. Retrieved from http://californiawatch.org/dailyreport/uc-berkeley-asked-absorb-80m-browns-500m-cut-8507

Frommer, F. J. (2009, July 8). Utah senator wants probe of BCS. *Southeast Missourian*. Retrieved from http://www.semissourian.com/story/1552991.html

Frontline. (2011, October 4). *The NCAA lawsuit*. Retrieved from http://www.pbs.org/wgbh/pages/frontline/money-and-march-madness/ncaa-lawsuit/

Gavora, J. (2002). *Tilting the playing field: Schools, sports, sex, and Title IX*. San Francisco, CA: Encounter Books.

Gerdy, J. R. (2006). *Air ball: American education's failed experiment with elite athletes*. Jackson, MS: University Press of Mississippi.

Gillum, J., Upton, J., & Berkowitz, S. (2010, January 15). Amid funding crisis, college athletics soak up subsidies, fees. *USA Today*. Retrieved from http://www.usatoday.com/sports/college/2010-01-13-ncaa-athletics-funding-analysis_N.htm

Giroux, H. A. (2007). *The university in chains: Confronting the military-industrial-academic complex*. Boulder, CO: Paradigm Publishers.

Giroux, H. A. (2009). Democracy's nemesis: The rise of the corporate university. *Cultural Studies ó Critical Methodologies, 9*, 669–695.

Giroux, H. A. (2010). Bare pedagogy and the scourge of neoliberalism: Rethinking higher education as a democratic public sphere. *The Educational Forum, 74*(3), 184–196.

Giroux, H. A., & Searls Giroux, S. (2012). Universities gone wild: Big money, big sports, and scandalous abuse at Penn State. *Cultural Studies ó Critical Methodologies, 12*(4), 267–273.

Harris, P. L. (2015, April 6). SJSU budget update. *SJSU Today: San José State University News*. Retrieved from https://blogs.sjsu.edu/today/2015/sjsu-budget-update-2/

Harvey, D. (2006). *Limits to capital*. London, England: Verso.

Hruby, P. (2013, March 19). The gold-plating of college sports. *Sports on Earth*. Retrieved from http://www.sportsonearth.com/article/42924176

Hums, M. A., & MacLean, J. C. (2004). *Governance and policy in sport organizations*. Scottsdale, AZ: Holcomb Hathaway Publishers.

Jones, R. (2015, January 18). Penn State still doesn't get it. *CNN*. Retrieved from http://www.cnn.com/2015/01/18/opinion/jones-penn-state-still-doesnt-get-it/

Judge, J., O'Brien, D., & O'Brien, T. (1995). Gender equity in the 1990s: An athletic administrator's survival guide to Title IX and gender equity compliance. *Seton Hall Journal of Sport Law, 5*, 313–338.

Jurewitz, R. (2000). Playing at an even strength: Reforming Title IX enforcement in intercollegiate athletics. *American University Journal of Gender, Social Policy and the Law, 8*(2), 283–351.

Katz, A. (2010, June 15). Source: Influential group saved Big 12. *ESPN*. Retrieved from http://sports.espn.go.com/ncaa/news/story?id=5286816

Kerkhoff, B. (2010, November 26). Big 12 problems trace to league's roots. *Dallas Morning News*. Retrieved from http://www.dallasnews.com/sports/college-sports/headlines/20100605-Big-12-problems-trace-to-league-5863.ece

Khan, S. (2012, August 9). Inside A&M's new training facility. *ESPN*. Retrieved from http://insider.espn.go.com/blog/colleges/tamu/post/_/id/485/inside-ams-new-training-facility

Khurshudyan, I. (2015, April 6). Dave Bliss gets a new college basketball coaching gig 12 years after Baylor scandal. *The Washington Post*. Retrieved from http://www

.washingtonpost.com/blogs/early-lead/wp/2015/04/06/dave-bliss-gets-a-new-college
-basketball-coaching-gig-12-years-after-baylor-scandal/

Kirp, D. (2003). *Shakespeare, Einstein, and the bottom line*. London, England: Harvard University Press.

LeRoy, M. H. (2015). How a "labor dispute" would help the NCAA. *University of Chicago Law Review, 81*, 44–66.

Loveridge, S., & Nizalov, D. (2007). Increasing the equity and efficiency of tax abatement programs. *The Journal of Regional Analysis & Policy, 37*(1), 10–14.

Low, C. (2012, June 14). Ranking the SEC's football facilities. *ESPN*. Retrieved from http://espn.go.com/blog/ncfnation/tag/_/name/2012-facilities-rank

Lyall, S. (2014, October 22). UNC investigation reveals athletes took fake classes. *The New York Times*. Retrieved from http://www.nytimes.com/2014/10/23/sports/university-of-north-carolina-investigation-reveals-shadow-curriculum-to-help-athletes.html

Maisel, I. (2014, August 8). Autonomy set to benefit athletes. *ESPN*. Retrieved from http://espn.go.com/college-football/story/_/id/11321434/autonomy-grants-power-5-more-control

Mandel, S. (2014, August 9). O'Bannon ruling deals crushing end to amateurism in NCAA athletics. *FOX Sports*. Retrieved from http://www.foxsports.com/college-football/story/o-bannon-decision-deals-decisive-end-to-amateurism-in-ncaa-athletics-080814

Marx, K. (1976). *Capital (Vol. 1). A critique of political economy*. London, England: Penguin.

Masterson, K. (2011, February). Donations to colleges rose, if only slightly, in 2010. *The Chronicle of Higher Education*. Retrieved from http://chronicle.com/article/Donations-to-Colleges-Barely/126178/

McIntire, M., & Bogdanich, W. (2014, October 10). At Florida State, football clouds justice. *The New York Times*. Retrieved from http://www.nytimes.com/2014/10/12/us/florida-state-football-casts-shadow-over-tallahassee-justice.html

Moore, D. L. (2005, June 8). Murder, scandal forced changes at Baylor. *USA Today*. Retrieved from http://usatoday30.usatoday.com/sports/college/mensbasketball/big12/2005-06-08-baylor-changes_x.htm

Mosco, V. (2009). *The political economy of communication* (2nd ed.). Thousand Oaks, CA: Sage Publications.

Mushnick, P. (2014, November 1). Media already quick to forget UNC academic scandal. *The New York Post*. Retrieved from http://nypost.com/2014/11/01/media-already-quick-to-forget-unc-academic-scandal/

National Collegiate Athletic Association (NCAA). (2014a). *About NCAA Division II*. Retrieved from http://www.ncaa.org/about?division=d2

National Collegiate Athletic Association (NCAA). (2014b). *Division II partial-scholarship model*. Retrieved from http://www.ncaa.org/about/division-ii-partial-scholarship-model?division=d2

National Collegiate Athletic Association (NCAA). (2014c). *Division III philosophy statement*. Retrieved from http://www.ncaa.org/governance/division-iii-philosophy-statement

National Collegiate Athletic Association (NCAA). (2014d). *NCAA Division I*. Retrieved from http://www.ncaa.org/about?division=d1

National Collegiate Athletic Association (NCAA). (2014e). *NCAA Division III*. Retrieved from http://www.ncaa.org/about?division=d3

National Collegiate Athletic Association (NCAA). (2014f). *2014–2015 NCAA Division 1 manual*. Indianapolis, IN: Author.

O'Toole, T. (2010, April 22). NCAA reaches 14-year deal with CBS/Turner for men's basketball tournament, which expands to 68 teams for now. *USA Today*. Retrieved from http://content.usatoday.com/communities/campusrivalry/post/2010/04/ncaa-reaches-14 -year-deal-with-cbsturner/1

Phillips, B. (2014, April 1). The Northwestern decision: An explainer. *Grantland*. Retrieved from http://grantland.com/features/northwestern-ncaa-college-athletics-union/

Pielke, R. (2011, November 24). Competing for TV contracts. *The New York Times*. Retrieved from http://www.nytimes.com/roomfordebate/2011/11/24/how-should-college-athletic -conferences-be-organized/college-football-is-a-competition-for-tv-contracts

Piketty, T. (2014). *Capital in the twenty-first century*. Cambridge, MA: Harvard University Press.

Porto, B. L. (1996). Suits by female college athletes against colleges and universities claiming that decisions to discontinue particular sports or to deny varsity status to particular sports deprive plaintiffs of equal educational opportunities required by Title IX. *American Law Reports, 129*(571), 1–14.

Prisbell, E., & Yanda, S. (2010, April 23). NCAA tournament to expand to 68 teams after deal is reached with CBS, Turner. *The Washington Post*. Retrieved from http://www .washingtonpost.com/wp-dyn/content/article/2010/04/22/AR2010042203916.html

Public Affairs. (2010, September 28). Chancellor announces new plan for Cal Athletics' future. *UC Berkeley News Center*. Retrieved from http://newscenter.berkeley.edu/2010/ 09/28/athletics/

Rauch, I. (2013, January 6). Here are a couple pictures of Johnny Manziel having a nice time at a nightclub after his Cotton Bowl win. *Deadspin*. Retrieved from http://deadspin.com/ 5973499/here-are-a-couple-pictures-of-johnny-manziel-having-a-nice-time-at-a-nightclub -after-his-cotton-bowl-win-updated

Redevelopment of Kyle Field. (2014). Retrieved from http://kylefield.com

Reich, J. B. (2003). All the [athletes] are equal, but some are more equal than others: An objective evaluation of Title IX's past, present, and recommendations for its future. *Penn State Law Review, 108*, 525–572.

Resnikoff, N. (2014, March 26). College athletes have the right to a union, labor board rules. *MSNBC*. Retrieved from http://www.msnbc.com/msnbc/college-athletes-have -the-right-union

Ritzer, G. (2011). *Globalization: The essentials*. Chichester, England: John Wiley & Sons Ltd.

Rovell, D. (2012, December 7). Will Johnny Manziel ever cash in? *ESPN*. Retrieved from http://espn.go.com/blog/playbook/dollars/post/_/id/2547/will-johnny-manziel-ever-cash -in#more

Rovell, D., & Gubar, J. (2013, August 6). Sources: NCAA investigating Manziel. *ESPN*. Retrieved from http://espn.go.com/espn/otl/story/_/id/9537999/otl-ncaa-investigating -johnny-manziel-profiting-autographs

Sablich, J., Fessenden, F., & McLean, A. (2012, July 23). Timeline: The Penn State scandal. *The New York Times*. Retrieved from http://www.nytimes.com/interactive/2011/11/11/ sports/ncaafootball/sandusky.html?_r=0

Salter, D. (1996). *Crashing the old boys' network: The tragedies and triumphs of girls and women in sports*. Westport, CT: Praeger Publishers.

San Antonio Express-News. (2014, December 29). Johnny Manziel's astounding family history. Retrieved from http://www.mysanantonio.com/sports/college_sports/aggies/item/Timeline-Johnny-Manziel-s-astounding-family-23035.php

Sander, L. (2011, October). NCAA approves scholarship increases and multiyear grants for athletes. *The Chronicle of Higher Education*. Retrieved from http://chronicle.com/blogs/players/ncaa-approves-scholarship-increases-and-multiyear-grants-for-athletes/29162

Schwartz, N. (2014, May 12). Texas A&M regent wants Kyle Field to be named "the house that Johnny built." *USA Today*. Retrieved from http://ftw.usatoday.com/2014/05/texas-am-kyle-field-house-that-johnny-built

Schwartz, N. (2015, January 17). ESPN's Keith Olbermann eviscerates Penn State. *USA Today*. Retrieved from http://ftw.usatoday.com/2015/01/keith-olbermann-penn-state-paterno-wins

Sen, A. (1983). Poor, relatively speaking. *Oxford Economic Papers, 35*(2), 153–169.

Shaw, P. L. (1995). Achieving Title IX gender equity in college athletics in an era of fiscal austerity. *Journal of Sport and Social Issues, 19*(6), 6–27.

Shulman, J. L., & Bowen, W. G. (2001). *The game of life: College sports and educational values*. Princeton, NJ: Princeton University Press.

Sigelman, L., & Wahlbeck, P. (1999). Gender proportionality in intercollegiate athletics: The mathematics of Title IX compliance. *Social Science Quarterly, 80*(3), 518–538.

Simon, R. (2005). *Sporting equality: Title IX thirty years later*. New Brunswick, NJ: Transaction Publishers.

Slaughter, S., & Rhoades, G. (2000). The neo-liberal university. *New Labor Forum, 6*, 73–79.

Smith, E. (2011, July 1). Will Lyles says Oregon paid him for "access and influence with recruits." *USA Today*. Retrieved from http://content.usatoday.com/communities/campusrivalry/post/2011/07/oregon-will-lyles-ncaa-investigation-yahoo-sports/1#.UMi09IM70WI

Smith, R. D. (2012). College sports' corporate arena. *Contexts, 11*(4), 68–69.

Solomon, J. (2014, December 23). Death of UAB football: Anger remains, but study banks on healing. *CBS Sports*. Retrieved from http://www.cbssports.com/collegefootball/writer/jon-solomon/24913760/death-of-uab-football-anger-remains-but-study-banks-on-healing

Sperber, M. (1990). *College sports inc.: The athletic department vs. the university*. New York, NY: Henry Holt Books.

Sperber, M. (2000). *Beer and circus: How big-time college sports is crippling undergraduate education*. New York, NY: Henry Holt Books.

Stafford, S. L. (2004). Progress toward Title IX compliance: The effect of formal and informal enforcement mechanisms. *Social Science Quarterly, 85*(5), 1469–1486.

Stephenson, L. (2013, February 28). Texas A&M VP Cook named "International Brand Master" by Educational Marketing Group. *Texas A&M Today*. Retrieved from http://today.tamu.edu/2013/02/28/texas-am-vp-cook-named-international-brand-master-by-educational-marketing-group/

Taylor, J. (2012, May 21). Big Ten's per-member payout this year? Nearly $25 million. *NBC Sports*. Retrieved from http://collegefootballtalk.nbcsports.com/2012/05/21/big-tens-per-member-payout-this-year-nearly-25-million/

Texas A&M Athletics. (2012, June 1). Countdown to the SEC: Why is Texas A&M joining the SEC? Retrieved from http://www.12thman.com/ViewArticle.dbml?ATCLID=205430546

Texas A&M Athletics. (2013a). Johnny Manziel bio. Retrieved from http://www.12thman.com/ViewArticle.dbml?ATCLID=205236136

Texas A&M Athletics. (2013b). Kyle Field redevelopment timeline. Retrieved from http://www.12thman.com/ViewArticle.dbml?ATCLID=208765870

Thelin, J. R. (1996). *Games colleges play: Scandal and reform in intercollegiate athletics.* Baltimore, MD: The Johns Hopkins University Press.

Thelin, J. R. (2000). Good sports? Historical perspective on the political economy of intercollegiate athletics in the era of Title IX. *The Journal of Higher Education, 71*(4), 391–410.

Tougas, F., & Beaton, A. (2002). Personal and group relative deprivation: Connecting the "I" with the "we." In I. Walker & H. Smith (Eds.), *Relative deprivation: Specification, development, and integration* (pp. 119–135). New York, NY: Cambridge University Press.

Tsitsos, W., & Nixon, H. (2012). The Star Wars arms race in college athletics: Coaches' pay and athletic program status. *Journal of Sport & Social Issues, 36*(1), 68–88.

Twitchell, J. (2004). *Branded nation.* New York, NY: Simon & Schuster.

Ubben, D. (2011, September 22). David Boren: Presidents agree to deal. *ESPN.* Retrieved from http://espn.go.com/college-sports/story/_/id/7006610/big-12-presidents-pledge-grant-television-rights-revenue-conference-according-oklahoma-president-david-boren

Upton, J., & Berkowitz, S. (2012, May 5). Budget disparity growing among NCAA Division I schools. *USA Today.* Retrieved from http://usatoday30.usatoday.com/sports/college/story/2012-05-15/budget-disparity-increase-college-athletics/54960698/1

Upton, J., Berkowitz, S., & Gillum, J. (2010). Big-time college athletics: Are they worth the big-time costs? *USA Today.* Retrieved from http://www.usatoday.com/sports/college/2010-01-13-ncaa-athletics-subsidies_N.htm

USA Today. (2012, May). *USA Today Sports' college athletics finances.* Retrieved from http://www.usatoday.com/sports/college/story/2012-05-14/ncaa-college-athletics-finances-database/54955804/1

Veblen, T. (1899/2007). *The theory of the leisure class.* New York, NY: Macmillan.

Veblen, T. (1901/2007). *Theory of the leisure class.* New York, NY: Oxford University Press.

Veblen, T. (1904/2005). *The theory of business enterprise.* New York, NY: Cosimo, Inc.

Vecsey, L. (2005, June 17). In Baylor tragedy, corrupt program should share in the guilt. *The Baltimore Sun.* Retrieved from http://articles.baltimoresun.com/2005-06-17/sports/0506170245_1_dotson-dennehy-baylor

Vint, P. (2014, March 27). Explaining what the Northwestern college football union decision means. *SB Nation.* Retrieved from http://www.sbnation.com/college-football/2014/3/27/5551014/college-football-players-union-northwestern-nlrb

Walker, I., & Smith, H. J. (2002). *Relative deprivation: Specification, development, and integration.* New York, NY: Cambridge University Press.

Walker, S. (1994). *The athletic department and the institutional development office: A systems approach to athletic fund-raising* (Doctoral dissertation). Retrieved from ProQuest Dissertations and Theses. (Accession Order No. AAI9434546). http://scholarworks.umass.edu/dissertations/AAI9434546/

Weather Channel. (2009, August). *Katrina's statistics tell story of its wrath.* Retrieved from http://xoap.weather.com/newscenter/topstories/060829katrinastats.html

Weaver, K. (2011). A game change: Paying for big-time college sports. *Change, 43*(1), 14–21.

Weight, E. A., & Zullo, R. H. (2015). *Administration of intercollegiate athletics.* Champaign, IL: Human Kinetics.

Wieberg, S. (2010, August). University of New Orleans athletics adjust to downsizing. *USA Today*. Retrieved from http://www.usatoday.com/sports/college/2010-08-26-hurricane-katrina-university-of-new-orleans-division-III_N.htm

Wiggins, D. K. (1995). *Sport in America: From wicked amusement to national obsession*. Champaign, IL: Human Kinetics.

Williams, J. J. (2001). Franchising the university. In H. A. Giroux & K. Myrsiades (Eds.), *Beyond the corporate university: Culture and pedagogy in the new millennium* (pp. 15–28). Lanham, MD: Rowman & Littlefield Publishers, Inc.

Wilson, J. (2015, January 30). UConn will offer enhanced athletic scholarships in fall. *Hartford Courant*. Retrieved from http://www.courant.com/sports/uconn-huskies/hc-uconn-full-cost-attendance-0131-20150130-story.html

Wise, M. (2003, August 28). College basketball; death and deception. *The New York Times*. Retrieved from http://www.nytimes.com/2003/08/28/sports/college-basketball-death-and-deception.html

Yost, M. (2010). *Varsity green: A behind the scenes look at culture and corruption in college athletics*. Stanford, CA: Stanford University Press.

Zimbalist, A. (1999). *Unpaid professionals: Commercialism and conflict in big-time college sports*. Princeton, NJ: Princeton University Press.

Name Index

Subject Index

A

AAUP. *See* American Association of University Professors (AAUP)

AIAW. *See* Association of Intercollegiate Athletics for Women (AIAW)

American Association of University Professors (AAUP), 23

Association of Intercollegiate Athletics for Women (AIAW), 11

Athletic funding crisis, NCAA Division I, 25–47; overview, 25–27; priorities, of universities, 36–45; pushback, 33–36; student fees, 31–33; tuition reallocation, 28, 31–33

Athletics in corporatized university: college athletics labor market, 62–67; corporatization in higher education, 49–53; "Johnny Football," 67–69; "keeping up" in college athletics, 59–61; overview, 48–49; at Texas A&M, 61–62

Athletics in higher education: corporatization of, 48–71; funding, 25–47, 74–78; history of, 1–24; new structure of NCAA, 84–85; unionization of college athletes, 80–82

B

BCS. *See* Bowl Championship Series (BCS)

Big East Conference, 45

Big Ten Conference, 4–7

Big Ten Network (BTN), 59

Bowl Championship Series (BCS), 59–60, 74–75

Branded Nation, 36

C

CAPA. *See* College Athletes Players Association (CAPA)

CBS, 21–22

College Athletes Players Association (CAPA), 85

College athletics labor market, 62–67

College Sports Inc., 40

E

Educational Marketing Group (EMG), 1

ESPN, 21–23

F

FBS schools. *See* Football Bowl Subdivision (FBS) schools

FCS schools. *See* Football Championship Subdivision (FCS) schools

Football Bowl Subdivision (FBS) schools, 9, 18

Football Championship Subdivision (FCS) schools, 9

H

Heisman Trophy, 66, 67

About the Authors

Jordan R. Bass, PhD, is an assistant professor at the University of Kansas. He has published numerous studies related to the funding issues within athletics and higher education. Specifically, Jordan has published relevant articles in the *Journal of Issues in Intercollegiate Athletics* and *Sport Management Review*. He also founded and serves as the coeditor of the *Journal of Amateur Sport*.

Claire C. Schaeperkoetter, MSE, is a doctoral research fellow at the University of Kansas. She is currently researching how the organizational structure and sociocultural dynamics of NCAA Division I and Division III athletic departments illustrate the role athletics play in the community at large. A former Division III student-athlete and national champion at Washington University in St. Louis, Claire provides a unique perspective having been both a Division III athlete and also an employee in a major NCAA Division I athletic department.

Kyle S. Bunds, PhD, is an assistant professor at North Carolina State University. Kyle has published multiple research articles related to the political economy of equitable development. Pertinent to the subject herein, he has published research in *Critical Studies in Media Communication* and *Communication, Culture, & Critique*. He also serves as an associate editor of the *Journal of Amateur Sport*.

About the ASHE Higher Education Report Series

Since 1983, the ASHE (formerly ASHE-ERIC) Higher Education Report Series has been providing researchers, scholars, and practitioners with timely and substantive information on the critical issues facing higher education. Each monograph presents a definitive analysis of a higher education problem or issue, based on a thorough synthesis of significant literature and institutional experiences. Topics range from planning to diversity and multiculturalism, to performance indicators, to curricular innovations. The mission of the Series is to link the best of higher education research and practice to inform decision making and policy. The reports connect conventional wisdom with research and are designed to help busy individuals keep up with the higher education literature. Authors are scholars and practitioners in the academic community. Each report includes an executive summary, review of the pertinent literature, descriptions of effective educational practices, and a summary of key issues to keep in mind to improve educational policies and practice.

This series is one of the most peer reviewed in higher education. A National Advisory Board made up of ASHE members reviews proposals. A National Review Board of ASHE scholars and practitioners reviews completed manuscripts. Six monographs are published each year, and they are approximately 144 pages in length. The reports are widely disseminated through Jossey-Bass and John Wiley & Sons, and they are available online to subscribing institutions through Wiley Online Library (http://wileyonlinelibrary.com).

Call for Proposals

The ASHE Higher Education Report Series is actively looking for proposals. We encourage you to contact one of the editors, Dr. Kelly Ward (kaward@wsu.edu) or Dr. Lisa Wolf-Wendel (lwolf@ku.edu), with your ideas.

The "Front Porch"

Recent Titles

ASHE HIGHER EDUCATION REPORT

ORDER FORM SUBSCRIPTION AND SINGLE ISSUES

DISCOUNTED BACK ISSUES:

Use this form to receive 20% off all back issues of *ASHE Higher Education Report*.
All single issues priced at **$23.20** (normally $29.00)

TITLE	ISSUE NO.	ISBN
_____	_____	_____
_____	_____	_____
_____	_____	_____

*Call 1-800-835-6770 or see mailing instructions below. When calling, mention the promotional code JBNND
to receive your discount. For a complete list of issues, please visit www.josseybass.com/go/aehe*

SUBSCRIPTIONS: (1 YEAR, 6 ISSUES)

☐ New Order   ☐ Renewal

U.S.	☐ Individual: $174	☐ Institutional: $352
CANADA/MEXICO	☐ Individual: $174	☐ Institutional: $412
ALL OTHERS	☐ Individual: $210	☐ Institutional: $463

*Call 1-800-835-6770 or see mailing and pricing instructions below.
Online subscriptions are available at www.onlinelibrary.wiley.com*

ORDER TOTALS:

Issue / Subscription Amount: $ _____

Shipping Amount: $ _____
(for single issues only – subscription prices include shipping)

Total Amount: $ _____

SHIPPING CHARGES:

First Item $6.00
Each Add'l Item $2.00

*(No sales tax for U.S. subscriptions. Canadian residents, add GST for subscription orders. Individual rate subscriptions must
be paid by personal check or credit card. Individual rate subscriptions may not be resold as library copies.)*

BILLING & SHIPPING INFORMATION:

☐ **PAYMENT ENCLOSED:** *(U.S. check or money order only. All payments must be in U.S. dollars.)*

☐ **CREDIT CARD:**   ☐ VISA   ☐ MC   ☐ AMEX

Card number _____Exp. Date_____

Card Holder Name_____Card Issue # _____

Signature _____Day Phone_____

☐ **BILL ME:** *(U.S. institutional orders only. Purchase order required.)*

Purchase order # _____
       Federal Tax ID 13559302 • GST 89102-8052

Name_____

Address_____

Phone_____ E-mail_____

Copy or detach page and send to: **John Wiley & Sons, One Montgomery Street, Suite 1000,
San Francisco, CA 94104-4594**

Order Form can also be faxed to: **888-481-2665**

PROMO JBNND

Great Resources for Higher Education Professionals

Student Affairs Today

12 issues for $225 (print) / $180 (e)

Get innovative best practices for student affairs plus lawsuit summaries to keep your institution out of legal trouble. It's packed with advice on offering effective services, assessing and funding programs, and meeting legal requirements.

studentaffairstodaynewsletter.com

Campus Legal Advisor

12 issues for $210 (print) / $170 (e)

From complying with the ADA and keeping residence halls safe to protecting the privacy of student information, this monthly publication delivers proven strategies to address the tough legal issues you face on campus.

campuslegaladvisor.com

Campus Security Report

12 issues for $210 (print) / $170 (e)

A publication that helps you effectively manage the challenges in keeping your campus, students, and employees safe. From protecting students on campus after dark to interpreting the latest laws and regulations, *Campus Security Report* has answers you need.

campussecurityreport.com

National Teaching & Learning Forum

6 issues for $65 (print or e)

From big concepts to practical details and from cutting-edge techniques to established wisdom, NTLF is your resource for cross-disciplinary discourse on student learning. With it, you'll gain insights into learning theory, classroom management, lesson planning, scholarly publishing, team teaching, online learning, pedagogical innovation, technology, and more.

ntlf.com

Disability Compliance for Higher Education

12 issues for $230 (print) / $185 (e)

This publication combines interpretation of disability laws with practical implementation strategies to help you accommodate students and staff with disabilities. It offers data collection strategies, intervention models for difficult students, service review techniques, and more.

disabilitycomplianceforhighereducation.com

Dean & Provost

12 issues for $225 (print) / $180 (e)

From budgeting to faculty tenure and from distance learning to labor relations, *Dean & Provost* gives you innovative ways to manage the challenges of leading your institution. Learn how to best use limited resources, safeguard your institution from frivolous lawsuits, and more.

deanandprovost.com

Enrollment Management Report

12 issues for $230 (print) / $185 (e)

Find out which enrollment strategies are working for your colleagues, which aren't, and why. This publication gives you practical guidance on all aspects—including records, registration, recruitment, orientation, admissions, retention, and more.

enrollmentmanagementreport.com

WANT TO SUBSCRIBE?

Go online or call: 888.378.2537.

JB JOSSEY-BASS
A Wiley Brand

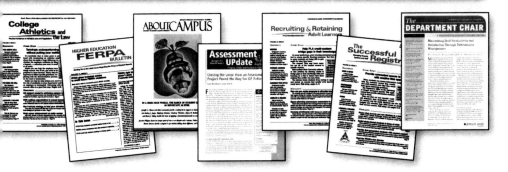